Motivating
Employees

Mr. Mark Whipple
5143 Britten Ln.
Ellicott City, MD 21043

D1114452

BEST PRACTICES

Motivating
Employees

BRINGING OUT THE BEST IN YOUR PEOPLE

BARRY SILVERSTEIN

Collins

An Imprint of HarperCollins*Publishers*

HarperCollins books may be purchased for educational,
business, or sales promotional use. For information,
please write: Special Markets Department, HarperCollins
Publishers, 10 East 53rd Street, New York, NY 10022.

The laws governing employer-employee relations differ
from state to state. The reader should be aware of the laws
in his or her state before taking any action that may affect
their employees.

Produced for HarperCollins by:

HYDRA PUBLISHING
129 MAIN STREET
IRVINGTON, NY 10533
WWW.HYLASPUBLISHING.COM

FIRST EDITION

ISBN: 978-0-06-114561-2

07 08 09 10 11   RRD   10 9 8 7 6 5 4 3 2 1

Barry Silverstein is a business writer and management consultant. He has 30 years of experience managing and motivating people in small and large businesses. He founded his own direct and Internet marketing agency and ran it for 20 years, growing it to a $5 million, 50-person organization. He also held management positions with Xerox Corporation and advertising agency Arnold Worldwide.

Silverstein is the author of three titles in the Collins Best Practices series. He is also the coauthor of *The Breakaway Brand* (McGraw-Hill, 2005) and the author of *Business-to-Business Internet Marketing* (Maximum Press, 2001) and *Internet Marketing for Information Technology Companies* (Maximum Press, 2001).

Contents

Preface

How do you motivate people? How do you get them excited about doing a great job? How can you inspire them to work harder? How can you recognize signs of de-motivation? Or, if you move into a new job and inherit a de-motivated staff, what tactics can you use to turn individuals around? How do you fire someone who refuses to cooperate? How do you keep your staff motivated and moving forward if your company is undergoing major change?

In this book, we distill the wisdom of some of the best minds in the field of management to tell you how to do a better job at motivating your people and creating an energized, motivated workplace that supports the goals of your company. The language is simple and the design colorful to make the information easy to grasp.

Quizzes help you assess your knowledge of motivational issues. Case files show how companies have tackled tough motivation problems. Sidebars give you a big-picture look at motivational challenges and highlight innovative, out-of-the-box solutions worth considering. Quotes from business leaders will inspire you as you face your own challenges. Finally, in case you want to dig deeper into the motivational issues, we recommend some of the most important business books available. The authors of these books both influence and reflect today's thinking about managing people, motivating them, and related issues. Understanding the ideas they cover will inspire you as a manager.

Even if you don't dip into these volumes, the knowledge you gain from studying the pages of this book will equip you to deal firmly, effectively, and insightfully with the motivation issues you face every day—to help you make a difference to your company and in the lives of the people who support you.

THE EDITORS

Understanding Motivation

"The only way to get people to like working hard is to motivate them. Every individual in an organization is motivated by something different."

—Rick Pitino,
NCAA basketball coach

Most people in business would agree that the best employees are motivated ones. Motivated employees are the individuals who take the initiative, who want to do good work, who move up the ranks, and who are generally the most likely to succeed.

Self-Assessment Quiz

ARE YOU A MOTIVATIONAL MANAGER?

Read each of the following statements and indicate whether you agree or disagree. Then check your score at the end.

1. I think motivating employees should be the responsibility of management.

   ○ Agree   ○ Disagree

2. I generally can tell when an employee lacks motivation.

   ○ Agree   ○ Disagree

3. I am honest and open in sharing essential information with employees.

   ○ Agree   ○ Disagree

4. I may be demanding, but employees know that they can count on me to support them.

   ○ Agree   ○ Disagree

5. I encourage employees to take ownership of their jobs and feel as if they are part owners of my organization.

   ○ Agree   ○ Disagree

6. I use positive reinforcement often with employees and present negative feedback in a constructive manner.

   ○ Agree   ○ Disagree

7. I care about employees as people and want to help them succeed.

   ○ Agree   ○ Disagree

8. I think it takes more than good pay to motivate employees.

   ○ Agree   ○ Disagree

9. Employees would say that I make them feel good about working in my organization.

   ○ Agree   ○ Disagree

10. Employees would say I inspire them to do their best.

    ○ Agree   ○ Disagree

Scoring

Give yourself 1 point for every question you answered "Agree" and 0 points for every question you answered "Disagree."

Analysis

8–10   You are an excellent motivational manager.

5–7   You could use some work on your motivational skills.

0–4   You have a lot more to learn if you want to motivate employees.

Employees who are motivated are loyal and dedicated and become ambassadors of good will for their companies. In fact, it's widely accepted that companies with motivated employees have lower turnover and tend to outpace their competitors in sales and profits. The more motivated your workforce is, the higher your organization's productivity will be.

> "Whenever anything is being accomplished, it is being done, I have learned, by a monomaniac with a mission."
>
> —Peter Drucker,
> management guru and author
> (1909–2005)

Motivating employees, then, is recognizing that employees are essential to the company's ability to succeed. It is about building a corporate culture of people who want to be exceptional at their jobs and who are proud of where they work. Motivating employees is not about giving people something they do not deserve or showering them with benefits and rewards so they will work longer hours or accept poor working conditions.

Behind the Numbers

DECLINING MOTIVATION

In about 85 percent of companies, employees' morale has been found to decline significantly after the first six months in a new job. It then continues to deteriorate for years.

A 2006 study showed that fair salary and benefits, the opportunity to accomplish good work, and satisfying relationships with coworkers are vital. If just one of these factors is missing, employees are three times less enthusiastic than employees at a company where all three factors are present.

Findings are based on surveys of about 1.2 million employees at 52 primarily Fortune 1000 companies from 2001 to 2004.

SOURCE: "Stop Demotivating Your Employees!" by David Sirota et al., *Harvard Management Update* (January 2006).

Although it is important to keep motivated employees motivated, the larger challenge for managers is finding out what motivates the *other* employees. Motivation is a very personal thing. What motivates some employees won't motivate others. Yet there are certain motivators with such wide appeal that most everyone responds positively.

This book will look at many of these motivators. We'll also discuss what it takes to be a motivational manager, how to keep employee motivation from falling, and why motivational leadership is essential.

> "Motivation is a fire from within. If someone else tries to light that fire under you, chances are it will burn very briefly."
>
> —Stephen R. Covey,
> author of *The 7 Habits of Highly Effective People*

As you consider how to motivate your employees, a basic understanding of the psychology of motivation is helpful.

The foundation of modern thinking about motivation is Abraham Maslow's "hierarchy of needs," introduced in 1943 and still used by psychologists, business managers, marketers, and others to understand what motivates people. Maslow theorized that after humans have met their basic physiological needs, they want to satisfy successively higher social and spiritual needs. Maslow identified four levels of needs above the most basic needs for food, sleep, and sex. Maslow's hierarchy is often shown as a pyramid, with the basic needs at the base, and the need for self-actualization at the tip of the pyramid.

Applying Maslow's theories in the workplace provides some insight into what motivates your employees. All employees express a basic concern for job security (the "safety" level of Maslow's hierarchy). Once their need for job security is fulfilled, employees will then look for

MASLOW'S HIERARCHY OF NEEDS

LEVEL 5
NEED FOR SELF-ACTUALIZATION
Opportunities for creativity, innovation, problem-solving, and learning

LEVEL 4
NEED FOR ESTEEM
Respect and recognition

LEVEL 3
NEED FOR LOVE AND BELONGING
Intimacy, friendship, family, religious group

LEVEL 2
NEED FOR SAFETY
Physical safety and freedom from threats, economic security

LEVEL 1
PHYSIOLOGICAL NEEDS
Food, water, sleep, sex

Dos & Don'ts ☑

MOTIVATION IS PERSONAL

It's your responsibility as a manager to keep your staff motivated.

☐ Do get input from employees about what they want before setting up a motivational program.

☐ Don't assume that every employee reacts the same way to a given motivational driver.

☐ Don't take a "my way or the high-way" attitude toward managing employees.

☐ Do let employees take ownership responsibility for their jobs.

☐ Don't fail to address lack of moti-vation as soon as you see it.

recognition and rewards for work well done (the "esteem" level). And if they feel both secure and recognized, they will be looking for job satisfac-tion (the "self-actualization" level), that is, the pleasure of growing within the job, the belief that the work is important to society, the sense that the work reflects the individual's values and goals. If you want engaged, motivated employees, make sure that they feel confident in their jobs; let them know you appreciate their effort, espe-cially when it has been extraordinary; and give them opportunities to learn and grow, to take on projects that would be meaningful (socially or personally) and that would put them closer to achieving their goals.

MOTIVATION ON THE JOB

In a recent study, described in the book *The Enthusiastic Employee: How Companies Profit by Giving Workers What They Want* (Wharton School Publishing, 2005), authors David Sirota, Louis A. Mischkind, and Michael Irwin Meltzer identify three goals sought by most workers. Employees want equity (specifically, fair pay, benefits, job security), achievement (that is, to be proud of their work and their accomplishments, and, by

Outside the Box

"IF YOU DON'T . . ."

It is remarkable what a difference wording can make.

Some managers naturally fall into using such phrases as "If you don't get that report done . . ." or "If you don't give me an answer today . . ." or "If you don't comply with the company rules . . ."

The "If you don't" phrase—often perceived as a threat instead of a request—is a universal turnoff. Next time, try turning the negative into a positive, as in, "I'd appreciate it if you could . . ." You'll probably see a very different reaction.

Behind the Numbers

AN UNDERAPPRECIATED WORKFORCE

Employees aren't adequately recognized or rewarded. Recent reports indicate that half of surveyed workers say they receive little or no credit, and almost two-thirds say management is much less likely to praise good work than to offer negative criticism when problems occur.

Research findings are based on surveys of about 1.2 million employees at 52 primarily Fortune 1000 companies from 2001 to 2004.

SOURCE: "Stop Demotivating Your Employees!" by David Sirota et al., *Harvard Management Update* (January 2006).

extension, praise, recognition, and growth on the job), and camaraderie (cordial relationships with coworkers).

None of these goals is particularly surprising in and of itself. After all, it is only common sense that workers desire fair pay, job security, and benefits. These basic needs, in fact, are represented in the "safety" level of Maslow's hierarchy shown on page 7.

Similarly, it's easy to understand that workers want to have good relationships with the colleagues with whom they spend so much time, or that they want to take pride in their work and accomplishments. It follows that, if employees

CASE *FILE*

MOTIVATION CAN BE FUN

Having fun in the airline industry? It just didn't seem possible until Herb Kelleher started Southwest Airlines.

Known for its corporate sense of humor, Southwest was long the major success story in an industry beset with bankruptcies. One of the reasons, says former CEO Kelleher, is the fun that management and employees have together. The airline is big on parties, often throwing award banquets to celebrate their people, complete with baby pictures and videos.

Southwest also has a personal touch. In 1966, the airline dedicated a plane to its 25,000 employees, listing all their names on the overhead bins. At corporate headquarters, employees' pictures line the walls. Every employee gets a birthday card as well as a card commemorating their anniversary with the airline.

It's all part of Kelleher's simple yet powerful philosophy: "We constantly do things that show our dedication and our gratitude to our people."

SOURCE: "Have Fun, Make Money" by Stephanie L. Gruner, *Inc. Magazine* (May 1998).

feel good about what they do at work, they will be more motivated to come to work the next day and do their best.

> "Nothing is worse for morale than a lack of information down in the ranks. I call it NETMA— Nobody Ever Tells me Anything."
>
> —Ed Carlson,
> former CEO of United Airlines
> (1971–1990)

What is startling about Sirota, Mischkind, and Meltzer's study is their finding that to maintain motivation among employees, *all three goals* must be met. In the absence of just one of them, motivation wanes dramatically. Although motivation is high for most employees when they start a new job, the study reveals, it drops dramatically after just six months and keeps dropping after that.

In other words, the stakes are high. If you don't address these three motivational issues right away, you will face consequences.

MOTIVATION IS MANAGEMENT'S ROLE

So what can a manager do to maintain a motivated workforce?

First, pay your people as well as you can. Do what it takes to provide benefits. Too expensive? Before you jump to that conclusion, weigh in the cost of hiring and training the constant round of new employees required to replace those who decide to leave.

Workers are frustrated by a lack of communication from management. Give them enough information to do their jobs properly and to make them feel respected and included.

Run an equitable workplace. Don't continue to pay people who don't pull their weight. Consider reward systems such as profit sharing based on individual and company performance. In some

• POWER POINTS •

WHAT EMPLOYEES WANT

Keeping in mind what motivates most employees is essential. Failing to address even one of these three factors will negatively affect morale:

- Fair treatment in pay, benefits, and job security

- The opportunity to achieve and take pride in one's work

- Good relations with coworkers

Dos & Don'ts ☑

HOW TO GET RESULTS

Motivating people takes work, but your efforts will be repaid with a more dedicated and loyal workforce, lower turnover rate, and higher productivity.

☐ Do create an environment of trust.

☐ Don't assume employees are naturally motivated.

☐ Do identify each employee's individual motivators.

☐ Do acknowledge good work often.

☐ Do make a big deal of special achievements and accomplishments.

☐ Don't let a new employee's enthusiasm wane.

☐ Don't restrict an employee to mundane tasks without responsibility.

☐ Don't keep an employee in the same job for too long.

companies, employees are given stock options; ownership provides a sense of responsibility that in itself can be self-motivating. In addition, don't forget intangible benefits, which don't cost you a cent, such as providing a bit of flexibility for a

☐ Do offer opportunities for learning and advancement.

☐ Do take every opportunity to broaden employees' jobs.

☐ Don't keep all the decision-making authority for yourself.

☐ Don't assume competitive pay solves motivational problems.

☐ Do make employees part of a team and foster cooperation.

☐ Do build employees' self-esteem by using praise instead of criticism.

☐ Do look for ways to have fun.

☐ Don't minimize the importance of good relationships with coworkers.

☐ Don't structure a rewards system that is inequitable.

parent who needs to take two hours off to see a child in a school play.

Second, don't treat employees as if they were disposable. Tread carefully around layoffs and reorganizations. Avoid them or handle them carefully if you can't: Remember that workers who remain with the organization will feel as if their lives and careers hang in the balance every time the company faces tough times. There is nothing more demoralizing

Third, make people feel good about their work on a daily basis. First, show them why their work is important and how it fits into a larger mission.

Second, give them feedback to let them know when they are doing a good job, and don't forget about formal quarterly, biannual, and annual reviews. Together, these will have a tangible benefit for you as an employer: By praising

CASE *FILE*

MOTIVATING WITH OUTSIDE BENEFITS

PR firm Metzger Associates wanted to reduce turnover. CEO John Metzger decided to allow his 30-plus employees to design a "Live Long and Prosper" program that focused on activities outside the workplace. They came up with four categories: physical fitness, outdoor living, relaxation, and education. Employees were reimbursed up to a set dollar amount for any activity they selected in each category.

In its first year, the program reduced turnover from 15 to 2 percent.

SOURCE: "Managing One-to-One" by Leigh Buchanan, *Inc. Magazine* (October 2001).

the kind of effort and performance you want to see all the time, you are teaching the employee to do a better job.

> "I have yet to find the man, however exalted his station, who did not do better work and put forth greater effort under a spirit of approval than under a spirit of criticism."
>
> —Charles Schwab,
> founder of Charles Schwab & Co.

Training over time will yield personal growth, which also promotes a positive attitude. Offer career advancement opportunities and the chance to learn. And don't throw up road blocks to accomplishment in the form of needless paperwork and approvals.

Finally, promote good feeling among employees whenever possible. Be alert for problems that arise with difficult people and take action. Promote opportunities for employees to get to know each other—such as company events that inspire employees and instill company spirit.

Foster projects that involve joint effort via work groups and teams. For you, the benefit is clear: According to many business writers today, teams can produce better work than individuals working alone.

> "It might be statistically more rare to reach greatness, but it does not require more suffering than perpetuating mediocrity. In the end, it is impossible to have a great life unless it is a meaningful life. And it is very difficult to have a meaningful life without meaningful work."
>
> —Jim Collins,
> author of *Good to Great*

What it comes down to is that nurturing motivation is one of management's most important roles. If management does not actively pursue ways to keep employees satisfied and productive, even those who are naturally motivated can lose their drive.

A motivated workforce does not just happen. Companies with a motivated workforce are managed by people who understand how to motivate others and work hard at doing that.

Respect for employees permeates the culture of many successful companies. Companies with a motivated workforce offer employees career advancement. They participate in the employees' careers and provide benefits that enhance the employees' personal lives.

Just as important, great companies with a motivated workforce encourage managers to work cooperatively as part of a team with their employees. Rather than distancing themselves from the rank and file, these managers are approachable, compassionate leaders. They may expect a great deal of the people who work for them, but they give as much as they get.

Essential Skill I
Being a Motivational Manager

"Motivation is the art of getting people to do what you want them to do because they want to do it."

—Dwight D. Eisenhower,
U.S. general and president
(1890–1969)

Some managers learn the hard way that they cannot motivate others if they themselves are not motivated. As a manager, you set the tone for the workplace. Your attitude permeates your work group. If you are enthusiastic, others will be as well.

If you are energetic, enthusiastic, positive, and assertive, your employees will pick up your style. If you practice self-motivation, it will be that much easier to motivate your employees.

This is not all it takes, however. A motivational manager also learns how to read his or her employees. The manager watches body language, evaluates behavior, and assesses performance. The manager gets to know what individual employees want and need. The manager understands each employee's motivators.

The motivational manager tends to be one step ahead of employees, anticipating what they might be feeling at any given time. The manager is sensitive, compassionate, and understanding. He or she can be demanding but does this without being harsh, abrupt, or authoritarian.

The motivational manager knows how to have fun with the staff. He or she may throw an occasional party, take everyone out to lunch, or hold some other surprise event. The manager recognizes employees who accomplish something by praising them publicly. If criticism of a certain behavior or performance is required, the motivational manager takes the employee aside and handles it in private.

The motivational manager rewards employees individually when appropriate, and as a group when warranted. Rewards may conform to company policy but are distributed equitably. An employee's loyalty, dedication, and hard work do not go unnoticed.

The motivational manager is also a motivational leader, one who instills confidence in

The BIG Picture

PUSHING THE RIGHT BUTTONS

Managers who know how to motivate their employees may not be trained psychologists, but they know a lot about human behavior.

Motivational managers recognize that each employee has a different motivational need. One employee might crave public recognition, while another responds to one-on-one encouragement. Motivational managers find out which buttons to push by observing their employees' personalities and learning what their goals are.

Most employees' buttons fall into a few basic categories, such as the desire for recognition, rewards, and the opportunity for advancement. By matching an employee to a category, and applying rewards already in place within an organization, a manager can create a powerful motivational experience for an employee.

employees and inspires them to succeed. Many employees will want to emulate a manager who has spirit and determination.

Being a motivational manager is not necessarily easy, but it creates the most dedicated, loyal workforce an organization can have.

BELIEVING IN OTHERS

Because employees' enthusiasm for their job typically wanes over time, managers must start the working relationship off with a bang, providing positive motivation from the get-go.

With new employees, a manager can immediately establish a motivational workplace by exhibiting personal enthusiasm and a positive attitude. Just as important, the manager must show that he or she trusts each employee.

> "The task of management is to make people capable of joint performance, to make their strengths effective and their weaknesses irrelevant."
>
> —Peter Drucker

Trust cannot occur without respect. The manager who respects every employee has an expectation that the employee will do the job well. The manager delegates work with confidence and does not micro-manage or meddle. The manager offers assistance when necessary but generally allows the employee the leeway and responsibility to get the work done.

Dos & Don'ts ☑

HOW TO STAY MOTIVATIONAL

Being the kind of manager who constantly motivates employees to work diligently and effectively is a matter of using certain good management techniques.

- ☐ Do exude energy and enthusiasm.
- ☐ Do practice self-motivation—it will be that much easier to motivate employees.
- ☐ Do anticipate what employees want and need.
- ☐ Don't be afraid to be demanding.
- ☐ Do respect your employees.
- ☐ Do recognize and reward employee loyalty, dedication, and hard work.
- ☐ Do create motivational events to keep your staff positive and involved.
- ☐ Don't criticize in public—keep negative comments private.
- ☐ Do offer public praise.
- ☐ Do instill confidence in employees and inspire them to succeed.

• POWER POINTS •

A MANAGER'S EXPECTATIONS

Having faith in your staff means delegating with confidence and not micromanaging. It is important to display the following key sentiments:

- **Trust** – You assign a task with the certainty that it will be done well.

- **Confidence** – You assume that an employee will perform to your expectations.

- **Respect** – You treat an employee the way you yourself would want to be treated.

By handling an employee in this manner, the manager is sending the signal that he or she believes in the employee. The cornerstones of that belief are trust, confidence, and respect.

Trust means giving the employee responsibility. It means believing that the employee will do the right thing—that he or she will follow policies and procedures and will accomplish the assigned task. Trust also involves trusting yourself enough to let go. It means understanding that while an employee may not handle things exactly as you would, you can accept that, as long as the end result is the same.

Confidence in an employee is based on your certainty that the individual will perform to your expectations. It means not worrying about tasks being completed correctly or on time. It means feeling comfortable that the employee will do what is necessary and right, even if you are not checking up on him or her. It is difficult to have confidence in someone else if you lack confidence in yourself.

Respecting employees means giving them the benefit of the doubt. It means treating each individual as you yourself would want to be treated.

Dos & Don'ts ☑

HOW TO SHOW YOUR RESPECT

Demonstrating that you value your employees involves treating them well every day.

- ☐ Don't ask an employee to perform an unpleasant task without providing a positive motivational reason.

- ☐ Do tell the truth about a company restructuring or layoff, especially if it is in an employee's department.

- ☐ Don't assume that showing strong leadership means giving a public dressing-down to an employee who has failed at a task.

- ☐ Don't lose faith in all your employees just because one of them has betrayed your trust.

CASE *FILE*

IN THE FACE OF TRAGEDY

Some 3,000 employees could have lost their jobs in 1995, after a fire destroyed Massachusetts-based Polartec-fleece manufacturer Malden Mills, a vestige of New England's once-thriving textile industry.

But third-generation owner Aaron Feuerstein did the unthinkable: He reached into his own pocket and company reserves to keep all 3,000 of his employees on the payroll with full benefits for three months—at a cost of $25 million. He considered his workers an asset, not an expense. Feuerstein became nationally revered for his leadership during difficult times and for his exceptional belief in his people.

Although the cost of rebuilding the plant, coinciding with a declining market and competition from low-cost imports, forced the company to file for Chapter 11 protection from its creditors in 2001, it is thriving today, largely because of major government contracts—which its skilled and experienced employees enable the company to fulfill.

SOURCES: "A CEO Who Lives by What's Right" by Mary McGrory, *Washington Post* (December 20, 2001).

The BIG Picture

A CLINICAL LOOK AT MOTIVATION

Motivation has long been studied by behavioral psychologists. In 1961, psychologist David McClelland suggested that human motivation was based on three dominant needs: the need for achievement, power, and affiliation. To measure those needs, McClelland co-developed the Thematic Apperception Test.

Subjects are asked to look at thirty-one images of different social and interpersonal situations and to make up a story about each one. Psychologists then interpret the stories to determine what they reveal about the person's needs for achievement, affiliation, and power. Today, the results of the test are used to suggest the type of job that would best suit that individual.

SOURCE: *Evocative Images,* edited by Lon Geiser and Morris I. Stein (The American Psychological Association, 1999).

It means being honest and straightforward. Respect also means recognizing an employee's efforts and rewarding an employee's loyalty, dedication, and hard work.

Trust, confidence, and respect may seem like basic concepts. But it is surprising how few

Plan B

BETRAYAL

On occasion, an employee betrays your trust. When that occurs, take corrective action immediately. Meet with the employee privately and provide specific feedback about how the individual let you down. Stay calm and objective, but let the employee know you are disappointed. Give the individual the chance to explain and to make amends. Work together to assure it does not happen again. If necessary, create a plan for improvement, and get the employee to agree to it.

managers really embrace them. The fact is, many managers themselves are not trusted or respected by their superiors, because their superiors may not believe in them. This is particularly true in highly structured organizations with many management levels, and in organizations run by self-made entrepreneurial owners who may have adopted an authoritarian or controlling attitude toward employees.

Another reason few managers operate on trust, confidence, and respect lies in the prevailing philosophy of modern American business. Today, when a company needs to improve productivity and profitability, reductions in staff are commonplace. When a merger takes place, one of the first changes is in the workforce; positions are eliminated and people let go.

When employees are regarded as a line item that can be cut at will, it is easy to forget that the workforce consists of individuals with unique skills and knowledge bases. Reducing salaries, cutting benefits, and laying people off becomes an impersonal means to an end.

Managers who must carry out the organization's orders to reduce staff under the above

Red Flags ⚑◆

WHAT NOT TO DO

Even when managers have the best of intentions, not following through on promises has a negative effect on their employees' motivation. Do any of these behaviors sound familiar?

- You tell an employee you will follow up on an issue but never do.

- You keep an over-qualified employee in a low-level position rather than making an effort to give him greater responsibility.

- You berate an employee in front of a group or at a meeting.

- You arrange a group event and then postpone it several times because "everyone is too busy."

Behind the Numbers

THE UNDER-MOTIVATED WORKFORCE

Keeping employee motivation high is a constant management challenge.

- 69 percent of operating managers called the "lack of employee motivation" the most annoying problem they face in their organization.

- 73 percent of employees said they are less motivated today than they used to be.

- 84 percent of employees said they could perform significantly better if they wanted to.

- 50 percent of employees said they are only putting enough effort into their work to hold onto their jobs.

SOURCE: *Super-Motivation* by Dean R. Spitzer (AMACOM, 1995).

conditions may become fearful of their own positions and take out their frustration on employees as a result. Alternatively, they may want to demonstrate to senior management that they are "tough" and can deal with cutbacks or layoffs decisively.

Unfortunately, managers who themselves are not trusted or respected may not trust or respect those who work for them. The cycle continues, unless some manager recognizes the vital role that trust, confidence, and respect can play in motivating employees—and moving the company from good to great.

Dos & Don'ts ☑

HOW TO GET YOUR MESSAGE ACROSS

When you speak to employees, your words carry a lot of weight—not only what you say, but also how you say it.

☐ Do be aware of how you speak and write—it makes a difference to employee motivation.

☐ Do use active listening in all conversations with employees.

☐ Do try to forestall the us-versus-them workplace mentality.

☐ Do speak clearly and at a comfortable, relaxed pace when addressing staff.

☐ Do use "you" and the person's name to warm your praise.

☐ Do say "I" when criticizing an employee to diminish the potential for argument.

☐ Don't forget to use body language to project sincerity, concern, and honesty.

COMMUNICATION

The way you communicate with employees can have a direct effect on their motivation. Your verbal statements, your body language, and your written communication all play a role in motivating employees.

The Importance of Listening

A common complaint among employees is that their managers don't listen to them. This is a

• POWER POINTS •

BODY LANGUAGE MATTERS

Nonverbal communication can be a powerful motivational tool.

- Eye contact expresses sincerity and holds the listener's attention.

- Smiling when you speak makes people want to focus on you.

- Relaxed arms and open palms suggest honesty.

- Leaning forward signals an attitude of acceptance.

- Leaning backward suggests doubt or resistance.

- Crossed arms, a furrowed brow, or lack of eye contact imply tension or disagreement.

The BIG Picture

LEARNING TO COMMUNICATE

Communication is so important in business that even great managers and leaders are coached at it.

Executive coaches are like personal trainers for business people. In addition to providing career and personal guidance, executive coaches often teach senior managers motivational communication skills. They coach executives in how to make better presentations, how to listen, how to avoid sending negative messages, how to differentiate between assertive and aggressive behavior, how to encourage cooperation, and more.

Ask if your company makes executive coaching programs available to managers or supervisors.

certain motivation-killer. One of the best ways to address this issue is to practice *active* listening.

Active listening focuses on the person who is speaking to you and shows that you understand what is being said. It almost always includes non-verbal cues, such as nodding, smiling, and other expressive reactions, as well as verbal cues and responses, including questions.

Active listeners process what someone else says, rephrase it in their own words, and replay it so the speaker can validate that the message was understood. It is a skill that requires some level of detachment, because your role as an active listener is to demonstrate understanding, whether or not you agree with what the speaker is saying.

Active listening can be particularly useful in any kind of verbal disagreement. It forces the listener to concentrate on what the other person is saying and to interpret it accurately. As a result, active listening can reduce conflict and avoid contradictory statements. When both

RECOGNITION BUILDS LOYALTY

Recent studies from the Business Research Lab, a national market research firm, point to a strong association between how long people intend to stay at a company and the recognition they receive there for good work. Notably, there is a strong correlation between the statement "I feel I am contributing to this company's mission" and the statement "This company gives enough recognition for work that's well done." So if there are staff members you particularly value, be sure to give them the praise and rewards they deserve.

SOURCE: Business Research Lab, www.busreslab.com (2005).

THE BOTTOM LINE

parties in an argument are actively listening to one another, they may be better able to reach a resolution.

CASE *FILE*

MOTIVATING WITH PASSION

One trait that makes some business leaders more motivational than others is their passion. In his book, *Pour Your Heart into It*, Howard Schultz, founder of Starbucks, speaks of his "passionate commitment to everything."

He writes, "When you're around people who share a collective passion around a common purpose, there's no telling what you can do." Not surprisingly, passionate company leaders motivate their employees to achieve great things.

Lou Gerstner did so when he turned around the fortunes of IBM, motivating his employees to work together to return the company to profitability. Steve Jobs also did so when he reinvented Apple, motivating his employees to build the consumer electronics company that launched the iPod.

SOURCE: *10 Simple Secrets of the World's Greatest Business Communicators* by Carmine Gallo (Source-Books, 2005).

Dos & Don'ts ☑

THE SECRETS OF MOTIVATING

Although what motivates people varies from one person to the next, certain behaviors affect everyone.

☐ Do get to know each employee's likes, dislikes, and talents and use this information to help find the person's motivators.

☐ Do offer public recognition for individuals who have performed at a high level or demonstrated outstanding dedication or loyalty.

☐ Don't view employees as the problem—get them involved in your organization's challenges and goals, so that they become the solution.

☐ Do hire the right people—those who fit your organizational culture, who want to work for you, and who are motivated to do a good job.

☐ Do find ways to maintain and reinforce the enthusiasm of your employees so it is sustained over time.

☐ Do challenge individuals to do their best at all times.

☐ Don't criticize someone's personality, lifestyle, or outside-of-work interests.

- [ ] Don't become argumentative, emotional, or arrogant when criticizing someone, and never verbally assault an employee.

- [ ] Do encourage individuals to give you honest input, then acknowledge it and act on it.

- [ ] Don't be so convinced that your way is the right way that you do not encourage and accept honest feedback and ideas from individual employees.

- [ ] Don't exhibit favoritism for one employee over another.

- [ ] Don't be indirect or vague when addressing a difficult issue with an employee.

- [ ] Do maintain eye contact and deliver a critical message in a way that's clear, direct, unemotional, and objective.

- [ ] Do offer constructive criticism as soon as a problem occurs—but do it in private.

- [ ] Do give the person being criticized a chance to tell his or her side of the story.

When you are speaking with employees, remember that your words carry a lot of weight. As a manager, you hold a certain power over employees and that can immediately establish an "us versus them" perception. It is therefore very important to be nonconfrontational, nonemotional, and objective. It doesn't hurt to have a sense of humor, either (although you should not make light of serious matters).

When praising someone, use the person's name and the word "you" frequently. When criticizing someone's performance or behavior, it is often best to change "you" messages to "I" messages to avoid the perception that you are verbally attacking the individual. For example, say, "I have a problem with not getting that report on time" instead of, "You were late with that report." Always focus on the specific behavior itself, not on the individual.

Body Language

Body language, or nonverbal communication, can be a powerful motivational tool. To project sincerity, concern, and honesty, maintain eye contact when you speak with someone. When you speak to a group, scan the faces frequently and make brief eye contact with several individuals.

Smile when you speak. If you are comfortable making hand gestures, do so with your arms in a relaxed position and your palms open. Point or make a fist only when emphasizing something important.

In a one-on-one conversation, you can practice nonconfrontational body language, as well

CASE *FILE*

PERSONALIZING EMPLOYEE MOTIVATION

Roy Pelaez manages over 400 people who clean airplanes for service provider Aramark. He needed to improve morale and reduce theft among his workforce, which is largely made up of immigrants, so he decided to get involved with his employees on a personal level.

Pelaez found government-subsidized babysitters to help workers who were single mothers; secured the services of a teacher to tutor his employees in English; and arranged for someone from the IRS to give free tax advice.

He also offered good worker incentives, such as a day off with pay to any employee with six months of perfect attendance and to anyone who turned in a wallet or pocketbook found on an airplane.

The results were stunning: a 12 percent reduction in turnover, the return of 250 wallets, and an increase in company revenue.

SOURCE: "How to Lead Now" by John A. Byrne, *Fast Company* (August 2003).

as watch for signals from employees. Leaning forward when seated communicates that you are interested or accepting of what is being said. Leaning back may express resistance or disinterest. Generally, crossed arms, hands planted firmly on a table, a furrowed brow, or lack of eye contact

Outside the Box

IT'S THE LITTLE THINGS

Complex recognition and rewards programs are not the only way to motivate your staff. Sometimes, it is the little things that count.

Recognizing an individual can be as simple as taking the time to stop by the person's office to say thank you, leaving a handwritten note on the person's chair, or giving the person a gift card as a token of your appreciation.

Great leaders make a habit of thinking of special, personal ways to recognize and motivate individuals.

convey tenseness or discomfort. These postures and movements in an employee suggest a lack of agreement with what you are saying.

Being aware of your own nonverbal signals, and reading the body language of others, can help you be a more effective motivator.

Sending Your Message in Writing

The power of the written word can be your friend or your enemy when it comes to motivating employees. A big problem in business today is e-mail. Managers and employees have become so informal and blunt in e-mail communications that an e-mail can often be misinterpreted or incite a negative reaction.

Do not write e-mails to employees in haste or anger. If you need to, write something down on paper, just to work off steam, then edit it and rewrite it as an e-mail. Never use capital letters in an e-mail—unless you want to seem to be SHOUTING.

"In motivating people, you've got to engage their minds and their hearts. It is good business to have an employee feel part of the entire effort. . . . I motivate people, I hope, by example."

—Rupert Murdoch,
CEO of News Corporation

Communicating in writing can work to your advantage, however, if you take the time to send a handwritten note or card complimenting or thanking an employee. This is a common and very effective technique that a number of business leaders use. It is perceived by the recipient as meaningful, both because you took the time to do it and because it is a very personal form of recognition.

MOTIVATING INDIVIDUALS

Motivating individuals starts with four small yet important concepts.

First, really listen to an individual employee. Never patronize him or her. Instead, encourage the person's input and act on it.

Second, understand an individual's unique motivators. They will be different for everyone. Once you understand what they are, tailor your interactions with the individual accordingly.

Behind the Numbers

PUZZLING RESULTS

In a group of adults who had worked on ten identical puzzles, all performed equally well. Half of them, however, were told that they had done a good job, while the other half were told that they had done badly. What were the actual results of a second round of testing with ten new puzzles? The group of people who believed they had been successful the first time really did score better—and the second group actually scored worse.

SOURCE: *In Search of Excellence* by Tom Peters and Robert H. Waterman, Jr. (HarperCollins, 1982).

Third, give your people responsibility and decision-making power so that they can be effective at their jobs. Trust that their own motivation will keep them going, and give them the support they need to succeed.

Finally, provide recognition and rewards when appropriate. Even more important, offer individual feedback on a regular basis.

Learn to Listen

A remarkable number of managers do not really listen to their employees. Most individuals know their job. A competent person can tell a manager how to be more efficient. Managers who invite employee input and take it seriously will find their workers to be more positive and more motivated.

Smart managers recognize an individual's passion and take advantage of it. For example, if an employee likes the detail of how things work, the manager could offer him an opportunity to analyze and improve the department's operations.

Give Responsibility

Managers who do not delegate effectively and who micromanage their employees' work are seldom pleased with the results. One of the best ways to motivate individuals is to give them full responsibility for getting their job done. A manager should provide direction and guidance, but not step-by-step instructions.

Give Feedback the Right Way

Employees welcome positive feedback, but sometimes managers can be stingy with it.

They simply don't take time to tell employees when they are doing a good job—and in so doing they miss the opportunity to motivate. The fact is that career growth keeps employees motivated, and responding to your input as their manager is one of the most important avenues of growth. The key is to provide feedback in the right spirit.

> "None of us is really as good as he or she would like to think, but rubbing our noses daily in that reality doesn't do us a bit of good."
>
> —Tom Peters and Robert H. Waterman, Jr., authors of *In Search of Excellence*

Positive feedback is motivational both for the receiver and the onlookers. It's important to deliver praise and positive feedback in public. That way, you demonstrate that you, as a manager, recognize and acknowledge effort and hard work. At the same time, praise highlights values you would like to encourage.

Giving negative feedback is another opportunity to motivate, although negative situations are always challenging. If an employee's behavior has provoked you, or you are angry or irritated (as you may well be), it is hard to remain impassive and matter-of-fact.

But remember that critical comments phrased in a negative way often put employees on the defensive and can cause them to tune out everything else you are saying, even if it's positive. The best course is to strive for dialogue.

Meet with the individual one-on-one as soon as possible after the problem has come to your attention. Adopt a respectful attitude—try to assume the best about the individual. Don't berate the employee and don't show your personal feelings lest you provoke an emotional response.

Stay focused on the goal of the conversation, which is to stop unwanted behaviors. Ask for explanations and their point of view, and make sure to practice active listening. Show empathy. Instead of dwelling on failure and undesirable behavior, concentrate on accepted standards.

Communicate what you would like to see instead, giving specific examples of positive conduct. Remind the person of performance goals you've previously worked out together. Then, approaching the negative situation as you would any problem, take a collaborative approach to solving it. Agree jointly on specific new goals that are measurable, action-oriented, realistic, and time-limited.

Set milestones—dates on which you will check in to see how work toward the goals is going—and follow up. Throughout the conversation, remember that constructive comments tend to spark action, and be as positive as you can.

Plan B

DON'T STAND IN THE WAY

If a team isn't functioning as smoothly as it should, the first thing to ask yourself is whether you are doing anything that stands in the way of the team's effectiveness.

Sometimes a manager unwittingly interferes with a team's progress by being overcontrolling. Even when inspired by a desire to help the team succeed, micromanagement can come across as a lack of respect and can suppress the team's creativity. Individual participants can become fearful of making a mistake. Make sure you are sensitive to your team's need for autonomy.

The focused attention from you as manager is motivational, as is working toward—and achieving—the right kind of goals. The best-case scenario is that you turn a poorly performing employee into a star.

MOTIVATING TEAMS

In the classic *Wisdom of Teams,* Jon R. Katzen-bach and Douglas K. Smith emphasize that it is a sense of common purpose directed at a clear compelling performance challenge that separates "extra-ordinary," or high-performance, teams from committees, councils, task forces, and other small work groups.

The teams highlighted by Katzenbach and Smith are energized because of their commitment to a goal that has been jointly created—and, in pursuit of that goal, by their accountability to each other even more than to management. The individuals on high-performing teams really care about their colleagues and about achieving their goals. Each team member derives individual satisfaction from membership on the team and feels that his or her role is essential to the team's

> "The combative or angry or critical, demeaning confronter does not solve problems but instead drives them more deeply into hiding."
>
> —Dr. Henry Cloud, author of *Integrity*

success. Individuals' self-esteem and pride become closely connected to the fulfillment of the team's mission. The sense of common purpose as well as the satisfaction of successes along the way motivate team members to further invest their time and creativity.

Dos & Don'ts ☑

TIPS ON MOTIVATING TEAMS

Fostering a spirit of collaboration and teamwork keeps team motivation high.

☐ Do define the team's mission and responsibilities.

☐ Do communicate a common sense of purpose.

☐ Do explain how the team's work supports your organization.

☐ Do model partnership and teamwork by being open and honest.

☐ Do make team assignments to take advantage of individual strengths.

☐ Don't assign a team member to a role if you are unsure it will suit him or her.

☐ Don't withhold information that could help the team accomplish its mission.

☐ Don't pit one team member against another.

☐ Do facilitate discussion and mediate conflict to keep discussions constructive.

Moreover, the team's enthusiasm is infectious: The productivity and positive results invigorates people outside the group as well as those on the team.

The single most important thing you can do to create this high level of energy and motivation is to outline clear performance requirements—for instance, to get a certain type of new product to market within a stated time period. Make the performance requirements specific to the team's goal, yet loose enough to allow team members to internalize and personalize them, and for synergy to work its magic.

Foster Cooperation

You can contribute to a team's success in several ways. First, as a manager, you must take care in choosing members with relevant and complementary abilities. Second, you must play a key role at the outset in motivating each and every individual to want to be part of the team. One way to accomplish this is by demonstrating that functioning as part of the team will yield a personal benefit, supplying the answer to the usually unspoken question, "What's in it for me?"

Third, as an equal member of the team, you will bring your own unique skill set. That may include a deep knowledge of a certain process, or abilities that enable you to encourage conversation among group members, or an understanding of each team member's individual strengths and how to draw them out. You can also model strong collaborative behavior yourself.

Stimulate Communication

The best teams never lose sight of their goals and consistently revisit discussions of the group's purpose, each time viewing it in terms of new information they have received while moving forward. You can help keep the goals and purpose top of mind. In addition, you can keep the

CASE *FILE*

SHARING CHORES

Eze Castle Software CEO Sean McLaughlin wanted employees to work as a team to keep a neater workplace. He assigned tasks on a rotating basis. McLaughlin himself did kitchen cleanup the first week.

The tasks took each employee only about 15 minutes each day. When everyone shared the effort, the workplace immediately became tidier.

McLaughlin also took a portion of the money he saved not having to hire administrative staff and put it into an employee fund.

By giving his team a shared purpose and letting them share in the benefits to the company, McLaughlin was able to get his group motivated even as they added this new responsibility to their day-to-day tasks.

SOURCE: "Managing One-to-One" by Leigh Buchanan, *Inc. Magazine* (October 2001).

ideas flowing. Practice active listening as your colleagues speak their opinions. Be honest and open yourself, and encourage frank dialogue and

> "The people who are doing the work are the moving force behind the Macintosh. My job is to create a space for them, to clear out the rest of the organization and keep it at bay."
>
> Steve Jobs,
> cofounder and CEO of Apple Computer

open sharing of information—remember that in many companies, people are conditioned to keep strong opinions to themselves. Often, everyday conversations in the workplace are focused on looking good to the higher-ups and not rocking the boat. That may mean avoiding conflicts and ideas that might appear edgy or harebrained.

In the team setting, you want to encourage ideas of all kinds. In addition, you should welcome conflicts of opinion, although you should be ready to facilitate a constructive discussion

• POWER POINTS •

"WHAT'S IN IT FOR ME?"

Motivating teams begins and ends with motivating individuals. Teams are most effective and motivation is highest when:

- Each individual wants to be a part of the team.

- Each team member feels that being a part of the team will be personally rewarding.

- Each individual member takes pride in fullfilling the team's mission.

- Each team member feels not only accountable to himself or herself for completing an assigned task, but also has a sense of accountability to the rest of the group.

that will lead the group to a consensus based on your common goals.

Praise individual team members for their collaboration, for their commitment, and for the contributions made by their independent thinking.

It's All About Us

T-shirts, coffee mugs, and other team logo wear remind team members of the goals and purpose they share and why it all matters. The strong personal feelings that develop as a result of sharing and resolving conflicts and working together to accomplish important ends is motivating in and of itself. Group social events, sporting events, and group activities are more meaningful as a result.

When you use devices like these as well as your own skills to foster collaboration, communication, and commitment in an atmosphere of caring and constructive conflict, you will soon see, in your team, the truth in the old saying that the whole is greater than the sum of the parts.

Essential Skill II
Dealing with De-Motivation

"People often say that motivation doesn't last. Well, neither does bathing—that's why we recommend it daily."

—Zig Ziglar,
motivational speaker

Managers need to be aware of both external and internal conditions that can contribute to the loss of motivation. Out of the control of most managers are external conditions, such as personal and family issues, that spill over into an employee's work life.

Financial pressures, health issues, relationship problems, and other personal challenges can distract an employee or reduce his involvement with work—and his motivation.

Within the workplace, any number of issues might impair motivation. Bad news associated with the reputation or financial condition of the employer could have an impact, as could uncertainty due to a merger or restructuring of the employee's organization, a reduction of pension or other benefits, or an increased workload without additional compensation. Disagreements with coworkers or the presence of less competent coworkers who are known to be paid more can affect morale. So can postponed performance reviews and a poor attitude toward employees on the part of management.

As a manager, you must do your best to create a work environment that limits the number of de-motivating factors. You can lend an ear to your employees and, by being flexible and understanding, help them through difficult times.

You can try to deflect organizational issues that damage motivation and morale, or at least explain them as best you can. Strong working relationships with employees in which you both guide them as individuals and work with them as part of teams also reduce the impact of negative situations.

HIRING TO REDUCE DE-MOTIVATION

Pharmaceuticals entrepreneur Ewing Marion Kauffman once observed that people who are motivated will motivate others. Because it's difficult to create that level of motivation, it's imperative to hire people with the capacity to be motivated about the business. If you staff your organization with positive, enthusiastic self-starters, you will have naturally motivated employees.

Employers who attract such employees tend to have managers who themselves are positive, enthusiastic, and happy to be the company's employee. Good working conditions, excellent benefits, and a reputation for integrity are motivational, as is the message that the organization

• POWER POINTS •

WHY DO EMPLOYEES LOSE MOTIVATION?
Both external and internal conditions affect employees and cause them to lose their drive.

Common factors outside the workplace
- Financial pressures
- Health issues
- Relationship problems

Common factors on the job
- Employer's financial problems
- A merger
- A reorganization
- Increased workload
- Disagreements with coworkers

Dos & Don'ts ☑

HOW TO KEEP MOTIVATION HIGH

Though you can't control every issue that affects your staff, you can minimize the impact of those that contribute to loss of motivation.

☐ Do form strong working relationships with your staff.

☐ Do create a work culture that is positive, rewarding, and fun.

☐ Do encourage employees to come to you with their problems.

☐ Do make sure your managers are caring and compassionate.

☐ Don't attribute all loss of motivation to workplace issues—be aware of personal issues.

☐ Do be on the alert for potentially motivation-killing working conditions, such as long hours and conflict with coworkers.

☐ Do consider a job candidate's personality and fit with your organization before hiring.

☐ Don't make a hiring decision without having others in your organization interview the candidates.

is successful, takes good care of its employees, and is a great place to work.

Lively recruitment ads can help attract the right people. Enthusiastic human resources recruiters help draw similar individuals at job fairs. Bonus programs encourage current employees to bring strong potential employees on board. The whole hiring process should focus on bringing you in the right type of worker.

> "People are not your most important asset. The right people are."
>
> —Jim Collins

Qualifications

When you make a hiring decision, it can have a strong impact on the morale of the rest of your staff. Make sure that every new hire is qualified for the position. Hiring someone who is under- or over-qualified for a job is sure to affect motivation—the motivation of others on your staff, and eventually that of the new employee who will either lack the skills and experience required to do the job, or, alternatively, be underchallenged.

Study the individual's resume closely to be sure it matches the requirements of the position. Consider not just the resume, but the cover letter. One that exudes enthusiasm for the position and the company is a good indicator of high motivation.

References and Interviews

When checking references, be sure to ask previous employers about an individual's motivation. Try to get input not only about strengths or weaknesses, but also about the individual's attitude and personality. Was this person a motivated self-starter who took the initiative, or did he or she always need to be told what to do? Did this person do more than was expected, or simply satisfy the minimum requirements? Is this someone coworkers respected and with whom they got along? Was he or she cooperative, engaged, and dependable?

In your interview, probe to find out what motivated each candidate in the choices they've

> "All the clever strategies and advanced technologies in the world are nowhere near as effective without great people to put them to work."
>
> —Jack Welch, former CEO of General Electric and author of *Winning*

made during their lives. As you ask questions about their decisions, their thinking style will come into sharper focus. Did the person find the motivation to take actions from within himself? Did she rely upon others to prompt an action? For each accomplishment on his resume, was the initiative to get the project or process started his own? Rather than formulating hypothetical questions about what a candidate might do under a given set of circumstances, use your candidate's resume to give you ideas for questions that elicit information about what he or she has done in the past—because research has shown that past behaviors are the best predictors of how people will behave in the future.

MISSION AND MOTIVATION

Once manufacturing-focused, American business today is increasingly service- and information-oriented. For many companies, intellectual capital offers a competitive advantage.

This is why your company's greatest resource is your people. People want to be part of an organization with a meaningful mission—an organization with integrity. People are highly motivated when they work for an organization that demonstrates by its actions that it believes in the value of its employees.

THE BOTTOM LINE

The BIG Picture

HIRING BY INSTINCT

It's a given that you should carefully consider each job candidate's qualifications for a position. However, your gut feeling about the candidate is just as important, so don't dismiss it.

You need to feel comfortable with the candidate as a person. Envision this individual in your organization: Can you see him or her interacting well with coworkers and superiors? Can you see the candidate accepting the company culture? Do you feel the individual's style is a good fit?

On these key points, don't make a decision based solely on your reason. Trust your instincts as well.

Formulate your questions carefully, also anticipating follow-up questions you might want to ask. Interview your strongest candidates personally, but also have a few others speak to them individually as well—asking the same questions that you have posed about prior experience, job qualifications, and management experience so that you can all compare notes. Avoid group interviews, which make many candidates uncomfortable. End by inviting the interviewee to ask you questions.

Knowledgeable questions, revealing that time has been spent finding out about your institution, demonstrate motivation as well.

Watch the candidate for signs of interest during the interview—an enthusiastic speech pattern, animated presentation, eye contact, smiling, nodding to display understanding, and active listening, with arms apart, gesturing with open palms, and a forward leaning posture.

After the interview, write down your impressions of the candidate right away—your gut feelings as well as your thoughts. Bring finalists back for second interviews to gather additional information and further assess their qualifications and motivational level.

Dos & Don'ts ☑

THE RIGHT STAFF

Growth follows when you start with the right people, ask the right questions, and stimulate them to produce.

☐ Do make sure that your recruitment ads are phrased to appeal to strongly motivated individuals.

☐ Do pick your most motivated employees to recruit at job fairs.

☐ Do encourage current employees to refer potential employees via a bonus program.

CASE *FILE*

UNORTHODOX MOTIVATION

Recruiter Jon Westberg of Lander International realized that he wasn't placing what he considered a sufficient number of candidates. The problem: He thought he might be devoting too much time to his outside interest in art.

CEO Richard Tuck, to whom he took his problem, startled Westberg by suggesting that he spend *more* time on his art and less time on the job. Tuck's recommendation was based on his feeling that, if Westberg was fulfilling his passion, he would become more energized and do a better job. Tuck has built an *Inc. 500* company with just such unorthodox thinking.

SOURCE: "The Right Staff" by Samuel Fromartz, *Inc. Magazine* (October 1998).

WHAT'S DE-MOTIVATING YOUR STAFF?

Before you can figure out why the motivation of a member of your staff is falling off, you have to be able to spot the signs. He or she may be missing work more often. He may seem to lack enthusiasm for everyday work or even new projects and may appear bored, distracted, or preoccupied. She may be uncharacteristically inattentive to details or erratic, losing her temper or having conflicts

with coworkers. Some employees who are losing their motivation are sloppy and disorganized
about their work area. Body language can be
another clue—furrowed brows, sad faces, vacant
eyes, clenched fists, or audible sighs.

Approaching the Employee

If you spot signs of de-motivation in one of
your employees, don't let the situation languish;
deal with it as soon as you notice it. Approach
the person in a nonthreatening way. Have a

Red Flags

WARNING SIGNALS

Watch for these danger signs that
motivation may be waning:

- Increased absenteeism

- Inattention to detail

- Apparent boredom

- General lack of enthusiasm

- Erratic behavior

- Distraction, apparent preoccupation

- Temper flare-ups

- Conflicts with coworkers

- Messy work area

- Negative body language

conversation in his or her own work area, if it offers privacy, or ask to speak in your office.

Be calm and unemotional. Begin by saying that you have noticed certain specific behaviors and mention what they are. Ask the employee what might be causing these behaviors. Ask if

The BIG Picture

THE FEAR FACTOR

Some managers still use fear to control employees. They may threaten to keep an employee after hours. They may announce an intention to dock pay. They may talk about withholding an annual raise or threaten to submit a poor performance review.

In the short term, this use of fear as a motivator may seem effective, and employees may toe the line. In the long term, however, fear usually turns to resentment—and a lack of respect for the manager.

Never does fear inspire the kind of effort that an employee who is motivated from within can put forth. Solid working relationships spark initiative, creativity, and the positive attitude that it takes to get things done. Over the long haul, fear is never effective.

Outside the Box

USE HUMOR

It has been proven time and again that humor helps maintain motivation and morale in the workplace.

A good sense of humor can diffuse anxiety and put people at ease. Friendly joking can lighten up a tense moment. (Of course, make sure it is appropriate.) Poking fun at yourself can make you seem more approachable.

In some organizations, humor plays an even more important role. Employee skits and outside improvisational troupes keep things light. For instance, Southwest Airlines founder Herb Kelleher, known for his self-deprecating humor, was famous among his staff for his Halloween costumes.

there are issues or barriers that are getting in the way of the person performing effectively on the job. Ask what you can do to help turn the situation around.

Encourage the person to talk to you. Be prepared to deal with anger or frustration. Some individuals have trouble describing what's wrong. Listen actively, and don't be judgmental.

Try to identify the issues that are causing the loss of motivation. Determine whether you can resolve them. Offer to help the employee in whatever way seems most appropriate. If the issue is personal, you might offer the option of a more flexible work schedule.

Dos & Don'ts ☑

HOW TO DEAL WITH MOTIVATION ISSUES

If you handle the motivation issue promptly, you may be able to stall the slide or even turn it around—and save yourself from losing a valuable employee.

- ☐ Do stay alert for signs of declining motivation.

- ☐ Don't wait to address an employee when you suspect a motivation problem.

- ☐ Do encourage employees to speak freely with you about problems.

- ☐ Do respond with compassion and objectivity.

- ☐ Don't be judgmental.

- ☐ Do try to offer a flexible work schedule or other reduction in work place pressure if the issue is personal.

- ☐ Do check in with the employee periodically if the problem can't be immediately resolved.

If the issue is work-related, you might be able to propose a solution. If you cannot offer an immediate resolution, promise the employee that you will get back to him or her. Set a deadline for doing so.

Following Up

Agree to follow up with the employee on the issue. Many times in a busy workplace, managers don't take the time to do so. Yet this seemingly simple action is more important than you might imagine. The consistent, sincere interest of a manager can make a big difference in an employee's attitude.

> "Management is nothing more than motivating other people."
>
> —Lee Iacocca,
> former CEO of Chrysler

Check in with the employee periodically. Do everything you can to find a solution to the problem. If the issue ultimately cannot be resolved, you can honestly tell the person that you did all that you could. Then you should continue to be supportive and helpful.

Dos & Don'ts ☑

INSPIRED MOTIVATION

Keeping motivation high among staff members is a matter of institutionalizing in your group the smart practices that have worked for good managers for years.

☐ Do lead your team in celebrating every success, large and small.

☐ Don't ignore organizational problems—deal with them openly and honestly.

☐ Do encourage employees to loosen up, have fun, and laugh.

☐ Do maintain an open door policy.

☐ Don't use fear in an attempt to improve an employee's performance.

☐ Don't promote intense competition among members of a work team.

☐ Do try to resolve a conflict between two coworkers by helping them to find a common ground.

☐ Don't tell employees you can resolve an issue affecting their morale unless you are certain that you have the ability to do so.

Reaching A Resolution

Once you have become aware of the issues that may be affecting an employee's motivation for the worse, it is important to try to resolve them.

Many employees are looking for someone who will listen and empathize with them. It is important to let employees "vent" to you without judging or criticizing them. This requires a certain level of detachment on your part. Even if you do not agree with the employee's perspective, you can do a lot of good just by listening.

When you move from listening to finding a resolution, you need to understand what role you can play. If the problem is of a personal nature, you can

Red Flags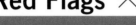

BEHAVIOR TELLS A STORY

Unresolved motivational issues can negatively affect employees' behavior. If you are alert for these warning signs, you won't be taken unaware:

- A change in attitude from cooperative to negative

- Minimal effort on the part of an employee who once did more than was required

- Silence and isolation from an employee who once interacted regularly with coworkers

go only so far. Your involvement must be limited to adjusting the employee's job responsibilities.

With a job-related issue, you must determine whether the issue is within your authority. A motivational difficulty that goes beyond your area of responsibility will be harder to resolve.

In this case, you will have to decide whether the issue also affects more than one employee and whether it is something you can legitimately bring up to senior management. If you know the issue will be difficult or impossible to settle, you should seek guidance from your boss. Then you will be able to tell the employee truthfully that you have made every effort to take care of the problem.

> "After you start doing the right thing, that's when the motivation comes and makes it easy for you to keep on doing it."
>
> —John C. Maxwell,
> author of *The 21 Irrefutable Laws of Leadership*

If the issue is within your limits of authority, determine whether anyone else is involved. If the issue involves a conflict with a coworker, the resolution you facilitate must involve

Plan B

SELF-RESOLUTION

Giving an employee the responsibility to handle a problem that is bothering him can be motivational in itself. Self-resolution can be especially effective with employees who lack self-confidence.

Before you make this choice, identify the issue at fault, and determine what information or resources might be needed to resolve the difficulty. Offer to collaborate with the employee—but give the individual as much freedom as you can to work through the issue. Provide guidance and support, holding periodic progress meetings with the employee until the issue is resolved.

both parties. Try to get the two individuals to appreciate each other's roles and find common ground. If they seem to be unable to work with one another, get them to concentrate on group goals rather than their own issues. In an effort to move their focus away from the dispute, for instance, you might give them both assignments that involve helping other team members.

If the issue is related to the employee alone, determine what you can do personally. If the problem involves the job responsibilities of the

CASE *FILE*

A WORKPLACE FREE OF RULES

A radical experiment called "Results-Only Work Environment" (ROWE) at electronics retailer Best Buy allows salaried employees to decide how, when, and where they work to accomplish what they need to get done. In this program, first implemented in 2002, the only measurement in evaluating employees is whether or not they successfully complete their work and meet the agreed-upon objectives they establish with their managers.

Sixty percent of Best Buy's divisional employees have converted to ROWE. Employees report better family relationships, higher company loyalty, and greater enthusiasm for the job. Statistics show the productivity of ROWE workers is 35 percent higher than that of employees not on the plan, and turnover is down more than 3 percent.

SOURCE: "Throwing Out the Rules of Work" by Patrick Kiger, *Workforce Management* (October 7, 2006).

individual, you may solve it by modifying or changing job responsibilities. If the difficulty is job performance, reviews, or advancement, evaluate how you can ameliorate the situation.

• POWER POINTS •

REVERSING DECLINING MOTIVATION

Resolving motivational issues will have a dramatic impact on morale. Various approaches can be successful:

- Some employees simply need someone to listen and empathize.

- Modifying or changing the individual's job responsibilities will solve some problems.

- To resolve conflicts among coworkers, get both parties to appreciate each other's roles and empower them to brainstorm their own solution.

If necessary, work with your superior or your human resources department.

Sometimes, working collaboratively with the employee to come up with an acceptable resolution is the appropriate course. Empowering the employee to play a direct role in resolving issues in itself may transform the unmotivated employee.

Ultimately, the time and effort you put into identifying and resolving the issues behind the falling motivation will pay off.

By encouraging employees to come to you about such issues, you will learn more about them—and about your organization. You will show yourself to be a caring manager, someone they can feel comfortable speaking to in confidence.

As a manager who knows how to turn an employee's attitude from negative to positive, you will potentially have a more satisfied, more motivated staff—and your organization will be better off as a result.

DIFFICULT SITUATIONS

When an employee's motivation wanes, you are bound to notice behavioral and performance problems. You will have to address the cause of the lack of motivation—and deal with the impact.

> "At first, you rarely succeed. Hence, you need to fail, fail again. My summa mantra goes like this: No big failures, no big successes."
>
> —Tom Peters

Lack of Confidence

An employee who is in the throes of a motivational crisis may well lack confidence or be afraid to make mistakes. When you discuss the problem, make an effort to be supportive and reassuring. Reiterate your faith in her abilities and your assurance that the setback is only temporary. Encourage him to keep trying and not to fear failure.

Lack of Cooperation

If an employee is uncooperative with you or with coworkers, call him on the behavior immediately. Do this in private and give specific examples in a way that's objective and calm.

Dos & Don'ts ☑

TURNING BEHAVIOR AROUND

Negative behavior and a lack of motivation are not necessarily permanent. Handled correctly, they can be reversed and the employee can be transformed into one of your star performers.

- ☐ Do use positive feedback and praise to bolster an employee's faltering confidence.

- ☐ Don't let the damaging effects of an employee's negativity on a work group go unaddressed.

- ☐ Do remind an unmotivated employee that lack of cooperation will prevent him from being successful.

- ☐ Don't neglect to reinforce positive behavior and strong performance.

- ☐ Do work with an employee to set objectives and timelines for correcting problems.

Explain that the refusal to be a team player hinders your group's performance and success. Ask the employee for his cooperation while the issue is being resolved.

Negativity

The negative mood of an employee with motivation issues can quickly spread through your staff. This affects the work environment and can damage group morale. If the employee is

> "The only way to deliver to the people who are achieving is not to burden them with the people who are not achieving."
>
> —Jim Collins

negative, point out the damage that the attitude could have on the work group. Encourage the individual to stay positive—or at least to remain professional—while you work on a resolution.

Disciplinary Action

If you have made a genuine effort to address an employee's unacceptable behavior or substandard performance during informal meetings and have not seen any change, you must take stronger action. When there has been misconduct, negligence, insubordination, unwillingness to perform job requirements, or similar just cause, issue a formal reprimand.

The first step in a progressive discipline process that could ultimately lead to termination is an oral reprimand. This is simply a discussion between you and an employee in which you define a specific problem and call for an action to correct it. Keep a record of the oral reprimand.

• POWER POINTS •

PROGRESSIVE DISCIPLINE

Take disciplinary action if you do not see any change in an employee's unacceptable behavior.

- Misconduct, negligence, and other just cause warrant a reprimand.

- Oral reprimands, which are given during a discussion, define the problem and call for a specific corrective action.

- Written reprimands restate the problem and the required action and formally put an employee on notice.

- Termination follows when the use of reprimands doesn't work.

If the undesirable behaviors continue to be a problem, take the next step and issue a written reprimand. This formally puts the employee on notice—and again documents the problem and calls for the action you previously requested orally. You should ask the employee to acknowledge the written reprimand by signing and dating a copy; file a copy with your company's human resources department. If the employee refuses to sign the reprimand, make a written note on the document.

"It's awful to fire people. But if you have a candid organization with clear performance expectations and a performance evaluation process . . . then people in the bottom 10 percent generally know who they are. When you tell them, they usually leave before you ask them to."

—Jack Welch

Reprimanding an employee doesn't require you to be angry or upset. In fact, your demeanor should stay calm, even if the employee becomes emotional. Remain firm yet fair as you explain the reprimands. Make it clear that you will take additional disciplinary action if the problem is not corrected.

If the reprimands fail to work, termination is warranted. Good written documentation of past unresolved problems is essential when you are ready to terminate someone. Be sure you have an adequate and justified reason. Be aware of your company's policy, and of any federal or state laws relating to termination.

Whatever the reason for the termination, deliver the news calmly and objectively. While the meeting should be private, it may be appropriate to have an HR representative present for support and as a witness.

An employee's reaction can range from disbelief to anger to an outburst of tears. Be compassionate yet firm; make it clear that the decision is final. Preserving an employee's dignity during a termination is the objective.

Essential Skill III
Rewarding Motivated Employees

"There's always the motivation of wanting to win. But a champion needs, in his attitude, a motivation above and beyond winning."

—Pat Riley,
NBA basketball coach

Most parents use recognition and rewards to encourage their children to behave well. The concept of recognizing and rewarding employees is essentially the same, with some important differences.

While the employer–employee relationship is somewhat parental, the employee works for pay. Pay and associated benefits rise as the employee's responsibility grows and job tenure lengthens. The competitive environment may influence remuneration as an organization strives to keep good employees from going to a competitor.

Pay and benefits are the foundation of an organization's recognition and rewards program,

CASE *FILE*

THE RIGHT REWARDS

At telephone headset manufacturer Plantronics, some 2,400 employees have continuous input into benefits and rewards via satisfaction surveys. The surveys have led to changes in Plantronics' training, retirement, and vision-care benefits.

S. Kenneth Kannappan, CEO of Plantronics, encourages employee involvement via both surveys and face-to-face encounters. He conducts monthly town-hall meetings and holds an annual management conference every summer. Kannappan believes employees' lack of motivation is due in part to management's failure to communicate.

SOURCE: "In a Former Life" by Ilan Mochari, *Inc. Magazine* (June 2001).

but they form only the baseline. Most human resources experts agree that an organization with a motivated workforce tends to be one in which recognition and rewards encompass more than these basics.

RECOGNITION VERSUS REWARDS

There is a distinction between "recognition" and "rewards." Recognition of an employee's efforts can come in the form of private words of thanks or public praise, via written notes or certificates of appreciation, or in other non-material ways.

Rewards are a specific form of recognition. In most organizations, rewards are monetary, or at least material. Must recognition always include material rewards to be motivational? This question is open to debate. Some research has shown that employees who receive praise or attention from their managers feel more appreciated and motivated than those who do not, whether or not material rewards follow. Other studies suggest money remains the strongest motivator.

Match Recognition to Objectives

Consensus does seem to exist about the need to link recognition programs to organizational priorities. Tying acknowledgement of an individual's achievement to specific objectives or performance goals is more effective than generalized recognition.

Involving employees in incentive programs matters as well. The most motivated employees are found in organizations that offer rewards in which the employees themselves have expressed interest, via opinion surveys, focus groups, or company votes. Such programs are far better received than those in companies that assume they know best what their employees want.

CASE *FILE*

OPPORTUNITIES YIELD PROFITS

When 29-year-old Tom Tiller was appointed head of GE Appliances' kitchen-range plant in Louisville, Kentucky, the situation was not a pretty one. No new products had been introduced in years, and plant employment had dropped from a high of 23,000 to 9,000. Tiller was faced with the need to lay off another 400 employees.

To counterbalance the negative effect of this action, he pulled 40 people from all areas of the company and put them on a bus to the Atlanta Kitchen and Bath Show. There, they carefully studied the competition and came back to the plant with a score of new ideas that yielded three new product introductions within 18 months and changed the bottom-line loss to a $10 million profit.

SOURCE: *The Leadership Engine* by Noel M. Tichy (HarperCollins, 1997).

Finally, it is crucial to recognize not only the big things, but also the little ones. Although exceptional performance deserves praise, only top performers are likely to receive it. In fact, an organization's success is the product of the modest but consistent achievements of the entire staff. These individuals merit recognition as well, if not on the same scale.

> "The purpose of a compensation system should not be to get the right behaviors from the wrong people, but to get the right people on the bus in the first place, and to keep them there."
>
> —Jim Collins

BARRIERS TO REWARDS SYSTEMS

Despite the fact that employee productivity reflects motivation, which rises and falls with recognition, organizations tend to throw up barriers that make it difficult to institutionalize the best practices of the company's most motivational managers. Each particular type of barrier is wrong in a different way.

Management by Exception

In high-stress environments, it is all too common for managers to claim that they only have time to deal with crises. During a crunch, they reserve their attention for employees who are having a problem or underperforming, at which time they swoop in and take decisive, corrective action. The basic attitude is, "If you haven't heard from me, it's because you're doing well."

Unfortunately, by making problem situations their priority, they completely ignore employees who are doing good work. It is almost impossible to build a rewards system in an organization whose managers do not take the time to recognize strong efforts.

"Throw Money at It"

In an organization with a money-solves-everything mentality, managers are encouraged to resolve every motivational or performance issue with money. Money, however, although a powerful motivator, cannot resolve fundamental and deep-seated problems—when, say, employees are always being asked to work overtime without compensation, or they clash with managers who are insensitive. In such situations, no added compensation can make up for the absence of job satisfaction.

"It's Not for Everyone"

Instituting a rewards system for a few star performers, or for a single department, is usually not wise. Your success rests on the shoulders of everyone in your company—not just the

CASE *FILE*

TRUE PERSONALIZATION

Marc Albin, CEO of Albin Engineering Services, Inc., believes his employees want to be recognized for different things, depending on their personal qualities, talents, and interests. He believes each person is different and therefore has different hot buttons.

At the end of orientation sessions, Albin e-mails each new employee and asks how he or she likes to be rewarded. Albin says his unconventional approach helps him understand what his employees "think of themselves and their abilities."

SOURCE: "Managing One-to-One" by Leigh Buchanan, *Inc. Magazine* (October 2001).

star performers. It is better to have a rewards system that is broad and all-inclusive and that uses levels of rewards to recognize levels of achievement. Similarly, a rewards system that is overly complex or has too many rules is doomed to failure. Preventing the system from becoming unnecessarily complicated is another good reason for employees to be directly involved in the creation of the rewards system.

"We Do Enough for Our Employees"

Some organizations think their employees should be grateful to have jobs and to be fairly

Dos & Don'ts ☑

ESTABLISHING A REWARDS SYSTEM

The wrong approach to a rewards system can backfire. Paying attention to these tips should help you motivate your employees and recognize their achievements:

☐ Do create a rewards system that is closely linked to your organization's priorities.

☐ Do recognize and reward the efforts of average employees as well as outstanding efforts by top performers.

☐ Do ensure fairness and objectivity.

☐ Do give impromptu rewards to keep employees from regarding rewards as entitlements.

compensated for them. Additional incentives above and beyond pay and basic benefits are unnecessary, the thinking goes.

In such organizations, employee motivation is apt to be low and the turnover rate high. Investing in even a modest rewards system can have a marked impact on productivity and employee retention. In fact, in some business environments, potential employees will look elsewhere if your level of benefits is not on a par with what other companies in the field are offering.

☐ Do allow employees to weigh in on the rewards system through surveys and focus groups.

☐ Don't exclude anyone from your rewards system by setting the bar too high.

☐ Don't assume that money is the only motivator that works.

☐ Don't implement a rewards system without associating recognition with rewards.

☐ Don't create a rewards system that is too rigid to be sustained over time.

SETTING UP A SYSTEM

In devising your rewards system, input from your employees is essential. Equally important, the system should be instituted consistently throughout the company. It should not only provide a way to reward worthy recipients on a regular basis but also allow for spontaneous recognitions. Surprising employees with occasional unanticipated rewards keeps the system fresh. As a result, employees will tend to view the rewards less as an entitlement and more as a privilege.

93

Plan B

WHEN REWARDS DON'T WORK

Rewards generally do not work when management misuses them. Recognition that is disingenuous or overdone can backfire. An "employee of the month" award can be ridiculed if it is not well deserved. Bonuses that are handed out to everyone at the same time each year may become perceived as entitlements and lose their effectiveness as rewards.

Be sure to keep rewards meaningful, special, and—at times—unexpected.

Whether impromptu or planned-for, all rewards must be distributed with fairness and objectivity. Individuals, teams, departments, divisions, and entire organizations can be recognized, but for most employees, singling out only a handful of organizational celebrities on a consistent basis tends to defeat the purpose of the rewards program.

A rewards system can have formal or informal levels of recognition as appropriate to specific accomplishments. Recognition itself can play an important role in the system if managers are taught effective ways to show appreciation. A face-to-face thank you, public praise, a handwritten note, or other impromptu gestures are legitimate ways to reward employees in small ways.

When you are assessing the need for a rewards system, be sure to look at it in the context of your existing benefits package. It may be that adding or improving benefits could constitute part of your rewards system. Pay special attention to nonmonetary possibilities—time off, improved working conditions, educational

DIFFERENT STROKES

Based on research conducted over the past five years, global professional services firm Towers Perrin has discovered that the qualities that initially attract people to a firm are considerably different from the qualities that make them stay. In a 2005 study, they found that the top driver of employee *attraction* to an employer in the U.S. was "competitive base pay," while the top driver of employee *retention* was that the organization nurtured employees who were motivated and had "the skills needed for the organization to succeed."

SOURCE: "Talent Management in the 21st Century" by Sandra O'Neal and Julie Gebauer, *WorldatWork Journal* (First Quarter, 2006).

THE BOTTOM LINE

• POWER POINTS •

REWARDING EXCELLENCE

A rewards system needs to be carefully thought out to be effective.

- Be consistent in rewarding employees throughout the organization.
- Solicit employee input.
- Give rewards as surprises to keep feelings of entitlement at bay.
- Avoid repeatedly rewarding only the top performers, which can de-motivate modest achievers.
- Offer an improved benefits package as part of your rewards system.

opportunities. Sometimes these are perceived to be even more valuable than monetary rewards.

The Real Value of a Rewards System

For most companies, the payback of a rewards system is simple: Employees who are recognized and rewarded feel valued by the company. This sense of being important to the group inspires job satisfaction and pride, which in turn—at least potentially—leads to sustained motivation. Even if an employee occasionally gets off track, the sense of being someone who matters to the organization is often enough to sustain a positive attitude.

On the other hand, a rewards system can backfire if it is constructed without the feedback and involvement of the employees. The whole plan to institute a rewards system may seem insincere, and employees may feel that the program is meant to recognize only the efforts of a select few. It can inadvertently send the message that the company respects just a handful of individuals and that every employee is not equally valued.

But when a rewards system is well designed and inspired by genuine appreciation for a company's employees, when it clearly represents the organization's goals, when it has a good balance of recognition and rewards, and when it

CASE *FILE*

REWARDING INNOVATION

Innovation is the highest priority at 3M, and a whole rewards system has been set up to encourage it. When a new venture is undertaken, the salaries and titles of everyone involved reward the work they put into it. A person who is a "first-line engineer" at the start of work on a new product, for example, becomes a "product engineer" when it is brought to market, then a "product line engineering manager" when sales hit $5 million, and so on, continually motivating people to strive for success.

SOURCE: *In Search of Excellence* by Tom Peters and Robert H. Waterman, Jr. (Harper Collins, 1982).

Outside the Box

PERFORMANCE INCENTIVES

If you establish a rewards system based on performance incentives, make sure the ground rules don't encourage abuse of the system.

For example, if you reward employees for reaching a new sales goal, make sure they are not doing so at the expense of the level of quality provided to existing customers.

While many performance incentive programs are well intentioned, they risk turning into a competition that harms service quality or even a company's reputation.

applies broadly across all employees and is based on fair and objective criteria, then the return on the company's investment in the program can be immense—a workforce that is more highly motivated, more satisfied, and more productive.

USING NONMATERIAL REWARDS

Nonmaterial rewards are as significant as material rewards in motivating employees—and in many cases, they can be more important.

A 1997 study from the Families and Work Institute indicated that "the quality of employees' jobs and the supportiveness of their workplaces are far more important predictors of these outcomes [job satisfaction, commitment, loyalty to employer, job performance, and retention] than earnings or fringe benefits."

The 2002 study from the same organization produced similar results: "When employees do receive more support in terms of flexible work arrangements, supervisors and managers who

> "I consider my ability to arouse enthusiasm among men the greatest asset I possess. The way to develop the best that is in a man is by appreciation and encouragement."
>
> —Charles Schwab

are responsive to their personal and family needs, and workplace cultures that are more responsive to work-life issues, they appear to be better employees—exhibiting higher job satisfaction, greater commitment, and more likely retention—and their personal and family lives benefit as well."

CASE *FILE*

HONORING THE RUNNER UP

Voyant Technologies honors employees who submit great new-product ideas. But the company's CEO, Bill Ernstrom, also acknowledges what he calls the "best almost-ideas."

Ernstrom recognizes runners-up with the "Elisha Gray Award," named for the inventor who waited too long to get a patent on his invention: the telephone. Ernstrom believes it is important to encourage future innovation from individuals who "thought differently enough—either correctly or incorrectly—to get somebody's attention."

SOURCE: "Hands On" by Anne Stuart, *Inc. Magazine* (August 2002).

Nonmaterial rewards are typically less expensive than material rewards and can sometimes cost the employer nothing at all. Ironically, however, they can be more difficult to implement, because they require a concerted ongoing effort by management to spend time with employees and pay attention to them. It isn't quite as simple as paying out a monetary reward.

Some managers simply do not know how to acknowledge an employee's contribution. They are not comfortable giving the pat on the back, whether it is a handshake, a kind word, or a thank-you note. Yet in many cases, a nonmaterial reward is simply that—an indication that a manager cares enough to take the time to express gratitude.

Immediacy and Sincerity Matter

Recognition or a nonmaterial reward should be given as soon as possible after an employee has exhibited the behavior or superior performance to be commended. The recognition should be specifically related to the event rather than generalized.

> "I've never known anyone to complain about receiving too much positive feedback. Have you?"
>
> —Jack Canfield,
> author of *The Success Principles*

It should also be warm, earnest, and sincere. Some managers make the mistake of conveying praise too quickly or even flippantly. Others praise or flatter too frequently. "You are doing a good job" loses meaning when it is not associated with a concrete achievement.

• POWER POINTS •

MANAGING NONMATERIAL REWARDS

To reap the benefits of nonmaterial rewards, managers need to:

- Understand that an environment responsive to work-life issues creates better employees.
- Appreciate that nonmaterial rewards cost less than material rewards so are good for the company overall.
- Encourage and act on employees' suggestions.
- Give nonmaterial rewards right away whenever they are deserved.
- Express their appreciation openly.
- Reward specific accomplishments.

The type of recognition matters less than the recognition itself. However, the expression of appreciation should suit the achievement. For example, a handwritten note is fine when an employee turns in a report ahead of a deadline, but as a thank-you for an outstanding effort on a major presentation, an informal lunch would be in order.

Types of Nonmaterial Rewards

Nonmaterial recognition can take several forms. An e-mail, a note, or a letter of thanks is always welcome. Bulletin board or intranet posts, or mentions in a company newsletter, are more public written expressions of commendation. You can also acknowledge an individual in person with a visit to his or her office or a lunch out. More publicly, you can praise the person at a meeting. Recognition devices, such as small gifts, company merchandise, gift certificates, or plaques are more enduring reminders. Or you can offer a one-time benefit,

Outside the Box

TRAINING REWARDS

Acquiring new skills and being exposed to new ideas is always stimulating. One great way to reward and energize employees whose performance you want to recognize is to send them to a seminar or convention—perhaps even with their spouse. Let them know that the trip salutes their achievements.

Then, via a memo, the company bulletin board, or the company newsletter, deliver the same message to the rest of the staff. Public acknowledgement and a new opportunity for personal growth will yield a more motivated and more loyal employee.

SOURCE: *Swim with the Sharks Without Being Eaten Alive* (Reissue Edition) by Harvey B. Mackay (Collins, 2005).

Red Flags ⚑◆

SINCERITY AT RISK

Insincerity and lack of support from a manager is de-motivating. Watch out for the following:

- False enthusiasm
- Patronizing praise
- Poor follow-through and unkept promises
- Personal complaints about workload to an employee

such as a day off or the opportunity to attend a workshop or seminar.

The Best Reward of All

Perhaps the best nonmaterial reward of all is not only recognizing an employee's current effort, but opening the door to the possibility of greater recognition in the future.

Most employees are highly motivated by the potential for advancement. One of the most powerful forms of recognition is an increase in an individual's job responsibilities—either additional challenges in his or her current position or opportunities to learn something new by cross-training with other departments or divisions.

Make the employee a team leader or have him or her supervise others. Offer the chance to work collaboratively with more senior team

• POWER POINTS •

MANY WAYS TO SAY "THANKS!"

Several forms of nonmaterial rewards may be appropriate.

One-on-One Recognition

- Handwritten notes and e-mails
- A personal letter
- Notation in human resources file
- Taking the employee to lunch
- Giving the employee a day off

Public Recognition

- Bulletin board or intranet posts
- Mentions in company newsletters
- Praise at staff or company meetings

Opportunities for Personal Development

- New work challenges—supervisory duties, a team-leadership position, the chance to set objectives and measure criteria for success
- The chance to attend a workshop or seminar

Recognition Devices

- A gift or gift certificate
- Awards, plaques

Behind the Numbers

THE COST OF DISENGAGEMENT

An employee engagement survey of the U.S. workforce conducted by Gallup in 2006 found that nearly 20.6 million workers, or 15 percent, are "actively disengaged" or fundamentally disconnected from their jobs. This translates into a cost to the U.S. economy of between $287 billion and $370 billion annually.

The research indicated that actively disengaged workers are significantly less productive, less loyal to their companies, and more stressed and insecure about their work than their engaged colleagues.

SOURCE: "Gallup Study: Engaged Employees Inspire Company Innovation." *The Gallup Management Journal* (October 12, 2006).

members, to set both objectives and success-measurement criteria, or to have input into important decisions.

If you find legitimate ways to turn a high-performance employee into a more valuable participant on your team, you as well as the employee will reap the rewards.

Look Inside Yourself

In the final analysis, nonmaterial recognition and rewards can be among the most powerful employee motivators. However, they will not be nearly as effective if the manager who bestows them is not respected by the employee.

To gain that respect, you must make a sincere effort to listen to employees, to believe that their opinions have value, to advocate for them and—yes—even to admit when you are wrong. This requires that you stop for a moment, look inside, and manage as much with your heart as your head.

Caring and compassionate managers who understand their employees' needs also understand what motivates and de-motivates each one. These managers intuitively realize the power of a kind word. They know that it takes more than money alone to keep employees satisfied.

"The individual who does not embody his messages will eventually be found out, even as the inarticulate individual who leads the exemplary life may eventually come to be appreciated."

—Howard Gardner,
author of *Leading Minds*

CASE *FILE*

NON-CASH MOTIVATIONAL REWARDS

According to a Northwestern University study of 235 managers, "Non-cash programs are more effective in achieving eight out of 10 corporate goals." That's why in 2005, Kelly Services, a Fortune 500 company specializing in staffing solutions such as temporary office help, introduced "Kelly Kudos," an incentive program that uses non-cash awards based on points to help increase productivity and retention. With Kelly Kudos, the company's 480,000 U.S. employees can accumulate award points over time to earn various kinds of merchandise. The company has found that employees who earn points in this program are generating three times more revenue than employees who do not participate in the program.

SOURCE: "Recognition That Resonates" by Charlotte Huff, *Workforce Management* (September 11, 2006).

USING MATERIAL REWARDS

Simply put, people work for pay, and while pay is not the only motivator, it is a significant one for most workers.

An increase in pay is the most basic form of material reward. In American business, it has become standard practice to increase pay annually. Typically, the only other time an individual's salary increases is when a raise accompanies a promotion. As a result, a pay raise is regarded as an entitlement, not as a reward.

> "Regular reinforcement loses impact because it comes to be expected. Thus, unpredictable and intermittent reinforcements work better."
>
> —Tom Peters and Robert H. Waterman, Jr.

Benefits provided by the company to the employee are also viewed as entitlements, which is unfortunate. A few years ago, there was a hue and cry among Microsoft employees when, in a cost-cutting effort, a favorite perk was eliminated—the clean towels that had been provided to employees who ran or bicycled to work or who exercised during the day. Employees at Boeing, also in Seattle, pooh-poohed the outcry, saying that they couldn't believe the lavishness of the package even without the towels. As their comments

Dos & Don'ts ☑

TIPS ON MATERIAL REWARDS

Material rewards are significant for their quality as well as for the recognition they imply.

- ☐ Do review your pay structure to ensure that it is competitive within your industry and geographic area.
- ☐ Don't implement a material rewards system without making a long-term commitment to it.
- ☐ Do add desirable benefits to your benefits package as the company grows and prospers.
- ☐ Do make sure the value of the material reward is appropriate to the employee's behavior, effort, or performance.

underscore, some companies' benefits are far superior to others, and this can and should be a legitimate motivator for an employee to join and stay with a company. Microsoft's newest employee initiative, MyMicrosoft, restores the towels and at the same time adds laundry and dry cleaning, grocery delivery from Safeway, on-premises convenience stores, Wolfgang Puck food to go, and discounts on housekeeping, yard care, auto repair, pet care, and other nonworkplace services.

- [ ] Do make sure any material reward is based on an outcome that an employee can achieve and control.
- [ ] Do consider alternatives to cash as material rewards.
- [ ] Don't rely solely on stock in a material rewards program.
- [ ] Don't assume cash or other material rewards will solve underlying issues that may be causing motivation to fall.
- [ ] Don't institute team rewards programs that create divisiveness or break down the cooperative spirit of a team.
- [ ] Don't make material rewards too selective and restricted.

The best way a company can turn benefits into motivators rather than entitlements is to continually remind employees of the value of those benefits. To do this, some companies send employees a report of the monetary value of their benefits at least once a year.

Benefits can also be improved or added as the company prospers. One motivational technique is to survey workers about the types of benefits they would like, and then implement some or all of those benefits if the company meets its performance objectives for the year. If employees associate the desirable benefits with company performance, and if they also understand the role they play in helping the company succeed, then benefits can become tangible rewards.

Individual Rewards

Outstanding effort or performance on the part of an individual employee may justify a special one-time material reward. A "spot bonus" of cash, a gift card, or some other type of material reward is a way to acknowledge an employee and motivate him or her to keep up the good work. If it is unexpected, it has even greater value to the recipient.

When you recognize an individual's effort with a material reward, it is often appropriate to acknowledge the individual publicly as well. Recognition connected to a reward is a very powerful motivator. The individual's achievement and reward can also inspire other employees. Make sure, however, that the individual effort is truly worth recognizing in a group setting. Otherwise, employees may resent instead of appreciate the recognition.

Team Rewards

Monetary and other material incentives can make the point that working as a team can be rewarding. Such rewards might take the form of prizes, vacations, bonuses, profit sharing, or stock options.

The key element is to distinguish team rewards from individual rewards. Having team members

CASE *FILE*

A SYSTEM TO STIMULATE CHANGE

When former General Electric CEO Jack Welch sought to spark and support entrepreneurial behavior all up and down the ranks, he targeted the compensation system—traditionally consisting of salary increases of 3 to 4 percent annually for all and yearly bonuses of 10 to 15 percent for most of the more senior people. The new system boosted salary increases and bonuses—to 10 to 15 percent and 30 to 40 percent respectively. And rather than handing them out solely to the people at the top of the corporate hierarchy, the new plan reserved rewards for the entrepreneurs and most effective managers in the company. This was the first step in completely redefining the fundamental bond between GE and its workforce.

SOURCE: *The Individualized Corporation* by Sumantra Ghoshal and Christopher Bartlett (HarperBusiness, 1997).

share in a bonus pool that increases as the team meets certain specific objectives is different from rewarding an individual salesperson who exceeds his sales quota. Any team reward should

The BIG Picture

REMEMBER THE OTHERS

It is likely that only 20 percent of your employees—if that—make outstanding contributions to your organization. This small percentage represents the few superstars who may exceed even your most aggressive objectives.

Although these employees should be rewarded, the others also merit attention. The 80 percent of your employees who work consistently, day in and day out, contributing in so many little ways to your organization's success, are important as well. Let them know you appreciate their efforts.

be equitably distributed in a way that does not favor one employee over another.

Remember that material rewards for teams should encourage and promote teamwork, not create divisiveness. The objective is to reinforce the notion that, by working as a team, individuals can reap benefits not otherwise available to them.

Some companies use the team rewards approach to establish friendly competition among work groups in an organization. While this may work in your organization, it is wise to proceed with caution. Pitting one team against another can indeed result in higher achievement, but it can also create an intensely competitive spirit that can turn teams against one another in

CASE *FILE*

BELIEVE IN YOUR PEOPLE

When the Brunswick Corporation went through a restructuring, morale was sinking. Then CEO Jack Reichert quintupled the authority to sign off on capital expenditures for everyone in the organization. For instance, the $100 expense that you once could approve became $500. According to Reichert, this left no question in people's mind as to whether they were trusted. After two years, Brunswick was a stronger, more productive company.

SOURCE: *Reinventing Leadership* by Warren Bennis and Robert Townsend (HarperCollins, 1997).

a ruthless effort to win. Additionally, be careful to set objectives that are not counterproductive. For example, if you establish a team objective related to a quantifiable number, be sure that the team is legitimately performing as required, not just focused on reaching that number for the sake of the reward. It is important to maintain a sense of greater organizational good if you choose to reward teams for competing with one another.

Company Rewards

A common motivational material reward at the division or company level is a bonus or profit-sharing program.

CASE *FILE*

HOTMAIL MILLIONAIRES

When Hotmail was in its developmental stages, twentysomething founder Sabeer Bhatia wanted to light a fire under his people. So, to communicate both the urgency of the project and his desire for big ideas—and to give everyone a stake in Hotmail's success—he gave out not $100 here or there but stock in the company. In less than two years, he had amassed 20 million clients and had sold Hotmail for $440 million. And as stock owners, fully half of his staff had earned millions for their contributions.

SOURCE: *It's Not the Big That Eat the Small . . . It's the Fast That Eat the Slow* by Jason Jennings and Laurence Haughton (HarperBusiness, 2000).

Typically, a profit-sharing program distributes payments to employees based on the organization's successful achievement of a financial or productivity objective. Since all employees contribute to that objective, each individual is eligible to receive a portion of the profit. Sometimes this portion is based on longevity or seniority. Profit sharing motivates individuals to work on behalf of the entire organization to get the maximum financial reward.

Stock options are another material reward that companies use as a motivational tool. A company can grant stock options as a "signing bonus," or tie the options to a combination of employee seniority and longevity. Typically, once an employee reaches a certain number of years of employment, the option to purchase stock, or receive stock without cost, can be exercised.

Stock can have a higher or lower perceived value than cash, depending on the financial strength of the company and the long-term performance of its stock. If the company is private, the stock may have a somewhat lower perceived value, because it cannot be sold on the open market.

Nonetheless, stock is a material reward that can be beneficial to both the company and the employee in that it represents a longer term commitment for both parties.

Material rewards, whether cash, goods, or stock, can be the foundation of an effective rewards system. But they can be even more motivational when accompanied by nonmaterial recognition that is genuine.

Essential Skill IV
Motivational
Leadership

"The leaders who work most effectively, it seems to me, never say 'I.' And that's not because they have trained themselves not to say 'I.' They don't think 'I.' They think 'we'; they think 'team.'"

—Peter Drucker

Leaders establish a vision, formulate strategies, scan the horizon for future problems and opportunities, generate ideas, and initiate new ways of doing things. Importantly, they also motivate employees.

Leaders do this by modeling the right behavior, setting high goals and standards for the company and for themselves, and displaying character and courage in their decisions and actions. The sense of purpose they exhibit, the image of a promising future that they paint, and the sense of urgency about the goals that can be achieved together make people excited about the company—and about them as a role model. In all of this, they motivate their followers to achieve.

Leaders can be found at all levels of a company, not just at the top. In *The Leadership Engine,* author Noel Tichy expresses the idea that the best companies actively develop leadership qualities up and down the ranks. As a manager, you are in a position to lead your group, but you have to earn the right—and the privilege. You do that by your contributions to the company.

You are consistently reliable; demonstrate intelligence, broad-mindedness, and a sense of fair play; show imagination and a willingness to innovate; and are direct and honest day in and day out. You support your colleagues and take the high road through conflict. You consistently exceed expectations. Through your actions, your colleagues learn that they can trust you. They come to have faith in your decisions, and know that you will always do the right thing, morally and ethically. Employees who feel that you are listening to them and employees who are learning from you are growing. And a growing, learning employee is, most likely, a motivated one.

Inspiring motivation in your staff yields loyalty and longevity. Without a strong leader, a business may plod along and never achieve greatness. But strong leaders who do all of these things make for stronger companies.

LEADING DURING CHANGE

Many people like to settle into a routine. They are comforted by the prospect of doing the same tasks tomorrow, in the same way, that they did today. They embrace the idea of a secure future

> "Leadership seems to be the marshaling of skills possessed by a majority but used by a minority. But it's something that can be learned by anyone, and taught to everyone."
>
> — Warren Bennis and Burt Nanus, authors of *Leaders*

in a known, static environment. They view the prospect of change as disruptive, difficult, and demanding. Change itself is de-motivating for these people.

Dos & Don'ts ☑

A CHECKLIST FOR LEADERS

Remember that having the title of leader doesn't make you one. First, you must earn the trust of your people.

- ☐ Don't lead without a vision.
- ☐ Do communicate your vision to your staff.
- ☐ Do present a long-range view of problems and opportunities.
- ☐ Do remain positive and upbeat.
- ☐ Don't hide bad news.

Yet in today's business world, with consumer tastes evolving and technology expanding our world with every passing day, change is also a constant. The Japanese, revealing their understanding that change is essential in order to better oneself, have a philosophy they call "kaizen"—continual improvement.

As a leader, it's up to you to make change the status quo, and to bring those who resist change—and that may be a significant portion of your staff—into alignment with those who are energized by it.

Resistance to change can take the form of complaining about the new boss or grousing about new rules and processes that change brings. Many

☐ Do recognize that people need to be managed as well as led.

☐ Don't assume that success energizes employees as it does you.

☐ Do empathize with employees struggling with growing pains.

☐ Do communicate frequently with employees to let them know their efforts will be rewarded—and follow up on your promises.

employees actually fear change, since it represents new, uncharted territory and a potential loss of control over the on-the-job aspect of their lives.

But powerful leaders draws even the most reluctant into the process of change. They encourage dialogue about change. They answer questions honestly and share information about plans for the future.

Highlighting the powerful positive aspects of change, they transform fear and resistance into acceptance. The goal setting and team work that are so integral to change provide opportunities for employees to stretch and broaden their skills, to take on new challenges—and to enjoy the satisfaction of doing good work and be rewarded for it. In this way, change can yield a host of motivational opportunities—and can energize the entire company.

Managing Change Is Possible

It is generally more difficult to be a leader than a manager. While you can acquire leadership skills, some of what you need to be a leader is deep down inside of you. You need to have the ability to express a vision. You need to have a good grasp of your own beliefs and values before you can inspire or motivate others. You also need to be a great communicator.

A situation of change draws on all these skills, as well as your managerial skills. You must deal with every individual, because one negative individual can sway the attitude of an entire work group, even if most of its members are positive or neutral.

John Kotter and Dan Cohen detail a multi-step change process in their book *The Heart of Change* (Harvard Business School Press, 2002) that could help leaders better prepare to lead and manage change.

First, establish a sense of urgency. Next, form a guiding coalition of change supporters, who will support and promote your initiatives. Third, create a vision—a picture of the future—and communicate it repeatedly, in many ways. Fourth, empower others to act on the vision. Fifth, realize that change takes a long time, so plan for and create short-term wins. Keep the momentum for change moving over time. Finally, institutionalize the new approaches

The BIG Picture

GETTING COMFORTABLE WITH RISK

Most change leaders are not averse to risk. Change brings organizational bumps, the potential loss of good people, and uncertainty about the future. However, the potential rewards often outweigh the risks.

Change leaders create a strong, clear vision, formulate a solid plan, and rally the support of others. They stay focused on long-term success, even when faced by temporary setbacks. All this minimizes the risk and keeps change moving in the right direction.

you have created during the process to make change "stick."

LEADING DURING GOOD TIMES

When an organization is doing well, it is usually in a growth situation. The organization is adding customers, increasing sales, and building profits. The growth may require adding more managers and more staff to do the work. Responsibility for training these new arrivals may fall on the shoulders of current employees and managers. While good times might seem enviable, they can be just as challenging as tough times for a leader.

Dos & Don'ts ☑

KEY SKILLS OF LEADERSHIP

Whether change and tough times are energizing or de-motivating has a lot to do with how they are viewed and handled by the company's leader.

- ☐ Don't isolate yourself.
- ☐ Do emphasize change as continuous.
- ☐ Don't give the impression that change will be easy.
- ☐ Do talk openly about the challenges of change, including the possibility of re-structuring or downsizing.
- ☐ Do encourage employees to ask questions and offer feedback, in good times and bad.
- ☐ Do keep your thoughts focused on your goals to keep your morale high.

New Demands

Growth might bring with it the need for employees to work harder to keep up with new business. It might mean employees need to learn new skills on the job. It might lead to some employees shifting to new responsibilities or new groups, or being assigned to new managers.

The result of growth could make it difficult to maintain the quality of service, or could even mean a loss of service quality, as the organization

☐ Do give employees the feeling that, although you may not have all the answers, you have a sense of how to get through tough times.

☐ Do recognize that challenging times will require sacrifices and unpleasant decisions.

☐ Don't create pictures that are falsely optimistic.

☐ Don't delay inevitable layoffs.

☐ Don't withhold information.

☐ Don't put individual employee issues on hold when dealing with company challenges.

attempts to meet customer demands. It might take longer to get things done because of new staff and more people involved in the process.

It is not unusual for an organization in the midst of such growth to find employees frustrated, angry, burning out, or losing their motivation. When employees are overworked or in a constant state of upheaval, they wear out. Even material rewards will do little to motivate them.

What You Can Do

It is crucial for a leader to balance his or her personal exhilaration with growth and success with empathy for the challenges facing the organization's workforce.

Good motivational leaders show compassion for their employees during growth periods. They urge the group to keep going and not give up. They try to institute improvements in working conditions to ease the stress.

In addition, they find ways to help employees lighten up and have fun. They remind employees

Dos & Don'ts ☑

CHANGE AGENT

There are ways to make the process of change go more smoothly.

- ☐ Do enlist a group of individuals as change supporters.

- ☐ Do put extra effort into creating and communicating your new vision.

- ☐ Don't assume everyone will embrace and understand the need for change.

- ☐ Don't try to implement change without a plan that includes both short- and long-term goals.

- ☐ Do remain as positive and enthusiastic as you want others to be.

that their efforts will be rewarded, and they help employees see that there is an end in sight.

A motivational leader is an effective general who leads employees to succeed. However, the leader also makes his or her presence known on the field of battle. Employees like to know that the leader is not just leading, but standing with them—in good times as well as in tough times.

The Greatest Gift

A leader's greatest gift is a motivated organization—people who are happy working as a

☐ Do demonstrate honesty, openness, and compassion during change, especially if it is painful.

☐ Do create short-term wins so people can continue to support change over the long term.

☐ Don't forget that change is a continual process that needs to be re-energized over time.

☐ Do bring everyone on board, so that each employee feels invested in a successful outcome.

Red Flags ✗◆

GROWING PAINS

Even when growth is your goal, achieving it can be disruptive and can hurt employees' motivation in the short term. Watch out for:

- Overburdened employees

- Employee burnout

- A decline in staff morale

- Apprehensiveness on the part of employees

coordinated, supportive team toward a common goal.

If you visit a motivated organization, you immediately sense the difference. There is a vibrant energy and a buzz of excitement. People seem to move as if they can't get where they are going fast enough. Positive enthusiasm pervades the atmosphere and there is laughter in the hallways.

These are the types of organizations that survive and thrive in the most challenging business environments. These are the organizations that succeed even in the face of adversity. Such motivated organizations do exist—but only when the leaders themselves are just as motivated.

It is the organization's leaders, from the supervisor to the department head to the division head to the CEO, who must inspire the company's employees and kindle their spirit.

It is great leaders who motivate employees to be great.

LEADING DURING DIFFICULT TIMES

Being a motivational leader when times are tough is a test of a leader's strength and positive attitude. The most challenging situation is a restructuring

> "If a manager wants to make the transition from manager to leader, he or she must actively seek out the good news and then publicly acknowledge those responsible."
>
> —Jason Jennings and Laurence Haughton, authors of *It's Not the Big that Eat the Small . . . It's the Fast that Eat the Slow*

or downsizing. Restructuring or downsizing inevitably means staff layoffs. Nothing can be more demoralizing and demotivating than the departure of coworkers. Bonds are broken and working relationships dissolved. The departing employees may be angry or resentful. Those who remain are sad to say good-bye to their colleagues but at the same time relieved to be spared—and apprehensive that they might be the next to go.

The departures are likely to increase the workload for the survivors. They may be asked to make sacrifices and to do more with less. Frozen salaries and reduced benefits, if they're a part of the picture, only exacerbate the situation.

Red Flags ✕◆

PLUMMETING MORALE

During tough times, employee morale can plummet rapidly. Look for these warning signs.

- Lack of interest and enthusiasm

- Frequent absences or requests for personal time

- Sadness over other employees being laid off

- Anxiety about employees' positions being restructured or eliminated

- Despair about the company's condition

- Skepticism about management's explanations of the situation

- Anger expressed toward coworkers or managers

Offering Hope

How can a leader motivate the workforce at a time like this? One of the most important things a leader can do is to be honest. Facts and decisions must be communicated honestly and openly. This is not a time to withhold information.

It's also key to let employees know that the management team is making every effort to solve the problem—but without implying that you have all the answers. You want to encourage employees to ask questions and to offer feedback. Then you need to consider the comments carefully, and respond.

Employees will be looking to you for direction and hope. Intuitively, they know that you cannot singlehandedly change business conditions or arrest declining sales. They do want to know, however, that you have a sense of how to weather the storm and navigate through the tough times.

As a leader, you yourself need to remain positive and motivated—no matter how hard that is. If your own morale is high, it will rub off on your employees, hard times notwithstanding.

OTHER CHALLENGES

Leaders face a whole host of other challenges. Perhaps the organization's entire industry is undergoing changes. Perhaps the company's turnover rate is very high. There may be revelations that the organization is being investigated or that a CEO or senior manager is leaving. Rumors of a merger or acquisition can also be challenging.

• POWER POINTS •

LEADING CHANGE

A leader has a big influence on how change is viewed in an organization. Certain points bear remembering.

- The status quo is an obstacle— most people don't want change.

- Employees must be shown the tangible benefits of change to embrace it.

- Leaders should prepare people for the continual possibility of change in business.

All of these scenarios constrain the leader's ability to motivate the workforce. Preoccupied with his or her own challenges, the leader may take the attitude that "employee problems will have to wait." However, it is at a time like this that employee issues are most pressing. Any organizational change or upheaval tends to have a more profound effect on the workforce than on the management. Leaders need to understand the implications of this reality.

Choose to Lead

Leaders meeting the challenges of business need to be the individuals that their organizations want and need. Sometimes, leaders will be forced to put others' needs first—to sacrifice time with their families and to deal with unpleasant decisions. Being a leader can be demanding. But the leader who is able to motivate people can attain immense rewards—most importantly the loyalty and friendship of the group of individuals who hold direct responsibility for the organization's success.

Off and Running >>>

You are now ready to put what you have learned from this book into practice. Use this section as a review guide:

CHAPTER 1.
UNDERSTANDING MOTIVATION

- What motivates some won't motivate all.

- After people have met basic needs, they want to satisfy higher needs.

- Employees' enthusiasm for a job falls off after six months.

- Even naturally motivated employees can lose their motivation if management does not nurture it.

- Motivation decreases turnover and increases productivity.

CHAPTER 2.
BEING A MOTIVATIONAL MANAGER

- Managers cannot motivate others if they themselves are not motivated.

- The motivational manager inspires employees to succeed.

- Trust, confidence, and respect are vital.

- Managers who trust and respect employees do not micromanage.

- Active listening shows you truly understand what is being said.

- Negative feedback can be valuable, if it is offered as constructive criticism.

- To motivate teams, establish a specific performance goal and nurture a sense of common purpose.

CHAPTER 3.
DEALING WITH DE-MOTIVATION

- The employer's financial problems, a merger, reorganization, increased workload, disagreements with coworkers, and other issues are de-motivating.

- A savvy manager minimizes the impact of negative influences.

- Hiring the right people helps delay declining motivation.

- A manager must always be alert for signs that motivation is waning.

- Good managers deal immediately with de-motivation.

Off and Running >>>

- Lack of motivation can yield undesirable behavioral problems that must also be handled.

CHAPTER 4.
REWARDING MOTIVATED EMPLOYEES

- Employees who are recognized and rewarded feel valued by their company.

- Some studies show that recognition motivates employees; others point to money as the strongest motivator.

- Praise your stars but remember that consistent efforts by average employees are essential to success.

- A rewards system must be fair and consistent to be effective.

- Nonmaterial rewards are effective but hard to implement.

- Recognition must be keyed to a specific event to be effective.

- Job advancement keeps motivation high.

- Nonmaterial rewards mean more when they come from a respected manager.

- Disciplinary actions are essential

if the negative behavior or subpar performance does not improve.

CHAPTER 5.
MOTIVATIONAL LEADERSHIP

- Good leaders are honest, confident, visionary, inspirational, intelligent, fair, broad-minded, courageous, straightforward, and imaginative.

- Change represents disruption and potential loss of control for employees.

- Good times can be just as challenging as tough times for a leader.

- Employees want to know that you have a sense of how to weather the storm and will help them get through the tough times.

- Effective leaders at all levels turn negative energy into positive energy and motivational opportunities.

Recommended Reading

The Transparent Leader: How to Build a Great Company Through Straight Talk, Openness, and Accountability
Herb Baum with Tammy Kling
In the wake of numerous corporate scandals, Baum offers business leaders a compelling method to get maximum results by being open and honest in business practices.

Leaders: Strategies for Taking Charge, 2nd ed.
Warren Bennis and Burt Nanus
Leadership guru Warren Bennis and coauthor Burt Nanus reveal the four key principles every manager should know.

On Becoming a Leader: The Leadership Classic, Updated and Expanded
Warren Bennis
In this best-selling classic, Warren Bennis discusses how great leaders have the ability to "unite people in a common purpose." This is a must-read for those seeking insight into motivating people to do their best.

Reinventing Leadership: Strategies to Empower the Organization
Warren Bennis and Robert Townsend
Two of America's foremost experts on leadership show how their strategies can lead organizations into a future that includes increased employee satisfaction and continued economic growth.

The Success Principles™: How to Get from Where You Are to Where You Want to Be
Jack Canfield with Janet Switzer
One of the coauthors of the incredibly successful *Chicken Soup for the Soul* series provides principles and strategies to meet a wide variety of goals.

Good to Great: Why Some Companies Make the Leap . . . and Others Don't
Jim Collins
This best-selling book distills research on thousands of companies down to eleven that did the right things to become great. It provides insight into how the heads of these companies motivated people to drive organizational success.

The Daily Drucker: 366 Days of Insight and Motivation for Getting the Right Things Done
Peter F. Drucker with Joseph A. Maciariello
Widely regarded as the greatest management thinker of modern times, Drucker here offers penetrating and practical wisdom with his trademark clarity, vision, and humanity.

The Effective Executive
Peter F. Drucker
Drucker shows how to "get the right things done," demonstrating the distinctive skill of the executive and offering fresh insights into old and seemingly obvious business situations.

The Essential Drucker: The Best of Sixty Years of Peter Drucker's Essential Writings on Management
Peter F. Drucker
A compilation of Drucker's key principles.

Innovation and Entrepreneurship
Peter F. Drucker
The business bible for presenting innovation and entrepreneurship as a purposeful and systematic discipline.

Management Challenges for the 21st Century
Peter F. Drucker
Drucker explains how businesses can reinvent themselves to retain relevance in our modern society.

Managing for Results
Peter F. Drucker
Drucker shows how to see beyond conventional outlooks and open up new initiatives that help grow your business and make it more profitable.

The Practice of Management
Peter F. Drucker
The first book to depict management as a distinct function, this classic Drucker work is the fundamental book for understanding this.

Corps Business: The 30 Management Principles of the U.S. Marines
David H. Freedman
Freedman examines the organization and culture of the United States Marine Corps and relates how business enterprises could benefit from such Marine values as sacrifice, perseverance, integrity, commitment, and loyalty.

The E-Myth Manager: Why Most Managers Aren't Effective and What to Do About It
Michael E. Gerber
Drawing on lessons learned from working with more than 15,000 small, medium-sized, and very large organizations, Gerber reveals why management doesn't work—and what to do about it.

Common Sense Business: Starting, Operating, and Growing Your Small Business in Any Economy!
Steve Gottry
This book tells you how to succeed in every phase of the small business life-cycle—from starting to operating, growing, and even closing down a business. Gottry offers practical applications in the real world of small business.

It's Not the Big That Eat the Small . . . It's the Fast That Eat the Slow: How to Use Speed as a Competitive Tool in Business
Jason Jennings and Laurence Haughton
This is an instructive text on how to create strategic planning and creativity to speed your business past the competition.

*What Really Works: The 4+2 Formula for Sustained
Business Success*
William Joyce, Nitin Nohria, and Bruce Roberson
Based on a groundbreaking 5-year study, analyzing data on
200 management practices gathered over a 10-year period,
What Really Works reveals the effectiveness of practices that
truly matter.

*The Wisdom of Teams: Creating the High
Performance Organization*
Jon R. Katzenbach and Douglas K. Smith
Katzenbach and Smith reveal what is the most important
element in team success, who excels at team leadership, and
why companywide change depends on teams.

The Five Dysfunctions of a Team: A Leadership Fable
Patrick M. Lencioni
Beginning with a real-life scenario, this insightful book
reveals how a CEO came to a company and built trust by
combating five specific team dysfunctions: absence of
trust, fear of conflict, lack of commitment, avoidance of
accountability, and inattention to results.

*Swim with the Sharks Without Being Eaten Alive: Outsell,
Outmanage, Outmotivate, and Outnegotiate Your Competition*
Harvey B. Mackay
In this straight-from-the-hip handbook, with almost 2 million
in print, best-selling author and self-made millionaire
Mackay reviews the secrets of his success.

Harvard Business Review on Motivating People
Brook Manville et al.
This book provides the perspectives of numerous thought
leaders on the challenges of motivating employees, from
articles that originally appeared in the *Harvard Business
Review.*

*You Can't Win a Fight with Your Boss: & 55 Other Rules
for Success*
Tom Markert
This guide to surviving the pitfalls of the modern corporate
environment presents 56 practical rules that you can use to
find corporate success.

Executive Intelligence: What All Great Leaders Have
Justin Menkes
In this thought-provoking volume, Menkes pinpoints the
cognitive skills needed to excell in senior management
positions.

*The Corporate Coach: How to Build a Team of Loyal
Customers and Happy Employees*
James B. Miller with Paul B. Brown
Founder and CEO of Miller Business Systems, Jim Miller
shows how giving customers legendary services and also
motivating employees make for a winning combination.

The HP Way: How Bill Hewlett and I Built Our Company
David Packard
David Packard and Bill Hewlett grew their company from
its start in a one-car garage to a multibillion-dollar industry.
Here is the story of the vision, innovation, and hard work
that built an empire.

*In Search of Excellence: Lessons from America's
Best-Run Companies*
Thomas J. Peters and Robert H. Waterman, Jr.
Based on a study of 43 of America's best-run companies
from a diverse array of business sectors, *In Search of
Excellence* describes eight basic principles of management
that made these organizations successful.

*Quiet Leadership: Six Steps to Transforming Performance
at Work*
David Rock
Rock demonstrates how to be a quiet leader, and a master
at bringing out the best performance in others, by improving
the way people process information.

*Mavericks at Work: Why the Most Original Minds in
Business Win*
William C. Taylor and Polly G. LaBarre
Fast Company cofounder William C. Taylor and Polly LaBarre,
a longtime editor at the magazine, profile 32 maverick
companies in an effort to examine the "most original minds
in business."

The Cycle of Leadership: How Great Leaders Teach Their Companies to Win
Noel M. Tichy
Using examples from real companies, Tichy shows how managers can begin to transform their own businesses into teaching organizations and, consequently, better-performing companies.

The Leadership Engine: How Winning Companies Build Leaders at Every Level
Noel M. Tichy
A framework for developing leaders at all levels of an organization helps develop the next generation of leaders. This enables a company to grow from within, which is the key to excellence, stability, and building team loyalty.

The Visionary's Handbook: Nine Paradoxes That Will Shape the Future of Your Business
Watts Wacker and Jim Taylor with Howard Means
In this book the authors show how nine paradoxes define the world's business and social climates.

Winning
Jack Welch with Suzy Welch
The core of *Winning* is devoted to the real "stuff" of work. Packed with personal anecdotes, this book offers deep insights, original thinking, and solutions to nuts-and-bolts problems.

Index

Make sure you have all the Best Practices!

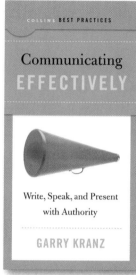

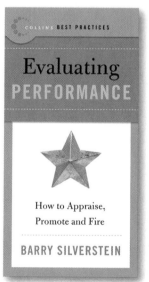

Make sure you have all the Best Practices!